TURNING TO GOD

TURNING TO GOD

Reclaiming Christian Conversion *as* Unique, Necessary, *and* Supernatural

DAVID F. WELLS

BakerBooks

a division of Baker Publishing Group
Grand Rapids, Michigan

12   13   14   15   16   17   18   7   6   5   4   3   2   1

To the memory of our colleague Klaus Bockmuehl,
whose passion for truth and righteousness
illumined our discussions.

Contents

Foreword

Many books have been written about conversion. However, David Wells's work, *Turning to God*, is unmatched in terms of its theological scope and richness, its cultural-anthropological perspectives, and its well-informed psychological insights. Wells weaves these factors together so as to make a persuasive case that Christian conversion is both supernatural and unique.

His message is of even greater urgency and importance to the global church today than when it was first published in 1989. The increasingly prevalent forces of pluralism and multiculturalism have shaped a mindset that is antagonistic to the exclusive nature of the claims of Jesus Christ, "I am the way, and the truth, and the life. No one comes to the Father except through me." Such claims of uniqueness are disparaged as arrogant and out of place in the twenty-first century. Exclusivity is an offence to the notion of tolerance, which is propagated as the supreme virtue of a globalized world. As a consequence, our churches are subtly altered by "believers" who are ambivalent on matters such as the authority of Scripture and the uniqueness of Christ.

In addition to the challenges that Christians face from those outside the church, we also deal with internal pressures to make the church more appealing and more accessible. Too often people are invited to come to Christ and to join the church in such a simplistic way that the process of "conversion" requires little by way of serious thought, little by way of a call to sacrifice, and little by way of a commitment to serve. Then one wonders why there is so little evidence of transformed lives, families, and communities.

When Jesus issued the Great Commission, he did not tell his followers to go into all the world and ask people *to raise their hands* or *to fill out a decision card*. Rather, he enjoined them to make disciples, baptizing them and teaching them to obey everything he had commanded. This requires an intensive and sustained investment in the lives of disciples, to the end that every aspect of a person's life is supernaturally converted and reoriented in turning to God.

Leaders of a new generation will be fortified as they benefit from the collective wisdom of those who have previously grappled with the question of Christian conversion in the modern world. David Wells wrote this book upon the completion of a Lausanne Consultation in Hong Kong in January of 1988. At that time, they were wrestling with influences of ecumenical theology that espoused social gospel theologies and that also envisioned a new world religion.

This Consultation on Conversion and World Evangelization, which was convened together with the World Evangelical Fellowship, brought together nearly fifty theologians, pastors, and mission leaders from around the world. Twenty-three papers were presented from a variety of perspectives, providing the basis for discussion and well-informed debate that was vigorous, respectful, and fruitful.[1] David Wells summarizes and interprets the findings of this consultation in the eight lucid chapters of *Turning to God.*

As this book is made available in a new version, it is with the prayer that it will embolden a new generation to regain or redouble their confidence in the truth that Jesus Christ alone is the Savior of the world, and that through their proclamation of this Good News, multitudes around the world will hear, repent, be saved, and indeed *turn to God.*

On a personal note, I would like to express my own sense of indebtedness to my friend and teacher, David Wells. It was during my last year in seminary that David began his distinguished teaching career at Gordon-Conwell Theological Seminary. His classes were as rich with his opening prayers and devotional reflections as they were with his lectures on Christian theology that would follow.

On one particular morning in October of 1978, Dr. Wells gave a devotional on the uniqueness of Christian service. He

1. Papers were presented in six areas. The first was biblical foundations, where we had the following papers: R. T. France, "The Bible on Conversion" (response by H. Blocher) and F. Foulkes, "The Conversion of Paul" (response by C. Horak). The second area was theological construction: J. I. Packer, "The Means of Conversion" (response by T. Engelsviken) and C. P. Choong, "The Place of Conversion" (response by J. Maeland). The third area was historical development: W. R. Godfrey, "Conversion in the Church to 1800" and P. Beyerhaus, "Conversion in the 19th and 20th Centuries." The fourth area was the psychological and sociological: Malcolm Jeeves, "The Psychology of Conversion"; John Court, "Psychological Factors in Conversion"; and Paul Hiebert, "The Sociology of Conversion." Fifth, there was the cultural context: E. Rommen, "Willowbank Updated"; K. Bockmuehl, "Christian Conversion and Marxist Culture"; Y. Eggerhorn, "Christian Conversion and Nominally Christian Culture"; Dennis J. Green, "Christian Conversion and Islamic Culture"; Mahendra Singhal, "Christian Conversion and Hindu Culture"; Milton Wan, "Christian Conversion and Buddhist Culture"; and Moishe Rosen, "Christian Conversion and Jewish Culture." Sixth, there was the missiological dimension: B. Nicholls, "Conversion and Baptism"; Joshua Yakubu, "Conversion and Pastoral Care"; Agnes Liu, "Conversion and the Urban Poor"; Suand Sumithra, "Conversion and the Cosmic Christ"; W. Stuckey, "Conversion and the Cults: A Case Study"; R. Buckland, "Conversion and Childhood"; and J. Engel, "Conversion and the Decision Making Process."

mentioned three factors. First, Christian service is unique in terms of the One we serve. We serve the living God. Second, Christian service is unique in terms of its demands. When Christ invites a person to come and follow him, he bids them come and die: *"Let him deny himself and take up his cross and follow me."* Third, Christian service is unique in terms of its rewards. *"There is laid up for me a crown of righteousness."* That devotional profoundly impacted me and it altered the trajectory of my life from that time forward. I realized afresh that my life was not my own and that I must deny my own dreams and ambitions to more fully turn to God. My life journey as a missionary of the gospel has been harder as a result. But my life's work in Japan and with the global church has been more gratifying and glorious than anything I could have imagined had I persisted with my plan. I thank God for using David Wells to help me understand the paradox of *finding through losing* and *living through dying.* The cumulative impact of his life has been to teach theology with the view that men and women will turn to God and enjoy the gift of forgiveness and the new life eternal that only Christ can give. Thanks be to God!

S. Douglas Birdsall, Executive Chair
The Lausanne Movement
Boston, Massachusetts
October 2011

Introduction

Conversions of all kinds are commonplace in our world today. An alcoholic turns from drink to sobriety. Westerners afflicted with boredom renounce their way of life and seek meaning from Eastern gurus. One person joins a cult and closes the door on his or her prior way of life; another looks for the power latent within and turns away from institutional religion.

Although these "conversions" may be precipitated by dramatic crises and result in changed behaviors, they are not conversions in any Christian sense. If they do not have Christ as their cause and object and his service as their result, they are not Christian. If they do not involve turning from sin to God, on the basis of Christ's atoning blood and by means of the Holy Spirit's work, they cannot be called Christian.

Then and Now

In 1988 when we met in Hong Kong to explore this theme, both the political and religious worlds were, in some respects, different from what they are today. It is worth looking back and thinking about what has, and what has not, changed in the two decades since then.

When we were meeting to think about this great Christian theme of conversion, the Berlin Wall was still standing, Marxism was dominating much of the world, and in Communist countries, Christianity was being severely repressed. Who could have seen that the next year, 1989, the Berlin Wall would be torn down and shortly after that the Soviet Union would implode? We certainly did not. Our thoughts were on the persecution of Christian pastors by atheistic governments in their unrelenting opposition to Christian faith. But in a moment, most of those governments were blown away as husks are by the wind. Were this book being written today, therefore, Marxism would not loom as large in its story as it does here, despite the fact that atheistic materialism still does have a formally sanctioned role in China.

The disappearance of the Soviet Union is not the only major change to have happened during this time. There have been many others. For example, the militant face of Islam was more obscured in the late 1980s. Were this book being written today, we would want to give even more attention to this religion than we did then. This is not simply because Islamic terrorism is often in the news, but because in our great cities, in both Europe and America, the Muslim presence is now so much greater than it was even two decades ago.

During this same time, the Christian world has also undergone significant internal changes. Today, the numerical center of gravity for the Christian faith is in the Southern rather than the Northern Hemisphere. This development was certainly underway in 1988 but now is completed. Indeed, Europe has largely divested itself of its Christian heritage, and often all that remains of a once-vibrant presence are empty cathedrals and churches. As a result of this demographic shift, the "face" of worldwide Christianity today is younger, browner, and less educated than it was in 1988. Even though this resurgent faith outside the West may be less informed, it is often more courageous than Western faith. Perhaps, were this book being written now, we would want to ask why this is and try to explain what has so weakened us in the West that our encounter with the modernized world has eviscerated our doctrinal belief.

This numerical and geographical shift in Christian faith is only part of the changing religious picture. Another aspect that goes largely unnoticed has to do with the massive waves of immigration, both legal and illegal, that have taken place. In the big picture, the pattern has been from the East to the West and from the South to the North. There are, however, important exceptions. Many people from the Middle East, for example, are moving westward into Europe, and most of them are religious. Their presence is keenly felt in many European countries but it is not a Christian presence. In America, many immigrants who have come from the East are either Christian or Hindu, and a few are Buddhist; many who have come up from South America are Catholic. As a result of this immigration and America's practice of freedom, today it is among the most religiously pluralistic countries in the world. This has brought to our own doorstep many of the religions that once were far off and were studied more as a curiosity than anything else. Today we must study them as a necessity; in that respect this book, which looks at these non-Christian religious competitors, has gained rather than lost practical relevance.

In 1988, we did not see the extraordinary change that was already underway throughout the West as it turned toward spirituality of every conceivable but non-Christian kind. Back then, we were very much focused on the West's secularism. This was not without reason. In the 1960s, it looked as though the West might become entirely secularized. Indeed, that was John Robinson's assessment in his 1963 book *Honest to God*. His contention was that Christians needed to adjust their faith to this changed circumstance or they would become completely irrelevant. A few years later, in 1966, *Time* magazine placed on its cover the bold question "Is God Dead?" This edition contained the account of a small band of radicals who, at that point, were almost entirely unknown—names such as Altizer, Van Buren, and Hamilton. They, too, had reached the same conclusion as Robinson and had already made their own internal adjustments. Nothing of Christian faith remained in their minds.

And so it was in the 1970s, especially in America, that the debate was joined with secular humanism. On the one side were the proponents of the old Enlightenment rationalism who expected that the day was not far off when all religions and spirituality would either wither away or at least be banished from American public life. On the other side were the religious who often feared that this was, indeed, the future into which they were staring. Thus it was that the struggle was joined.

However, things did not turn out exactly as either side imagined. The secular impulse clearly has persisted and is especially virulent in certain pockets of society. It has found a home among the cultural elites in particular, those who produce the symbols, language, and images by which we understand ourselves. But among more ordinary people, something entirely different was happening and very few saw it coming. Side-by-side with this secular outlook has sprung up a spiritual yearning. The transformation was complete by the 1990s. At the end of this decade, eight out of ten Americans said they were "spiritual," and that number was duplicated in Britain. Of these, a third said that they were "spiritual but not religious." By that they meant that they would not consent to believing doctrines that had been formulated by others from a source they did not accept as authoritative, such as the Bible. Nor would they feel bound to be part of any religious group such as a church. And they would not accept ethical rules that they had not devised and formulated for themselves.

In 1988, we did not see this development coming, nor could we have seen how ubiquitous technology would become, especially the internet, which would facilitate this privatized search for the spiritual. Today, evangelicalism is acutely vulnerable to this impulse, its weakness signaled by the underlying distaste for doctrinal understanding, for the place of the local church, and for seeing biblical ethical norms as absolute. It may well be that this cultural spirituality will pose an even greater threat to biblical faith than the secularism and Marxism that we thought about so hard during this consultation in Hong Kong two decades ago. The reason is that on the surface these cultural spiritualities—which take many different forms, including Zen, sanitized (Western) Hinduism, Kabbalah, mystical paganism with its many varieties of pantheism—offer what Christian faith offers. They imitate it and even have their own versions of conversion. Despite appearances, however, they are not variations on Christian faith but alternatives to it. They are its enemy.

It is salutary to look back on the theologies that we engaged in 1988. Then, they were dominant; today, most have shriveled or disappeared entirely. The World Council of Churches, which played host to many of these and offered its various forums for their propagation, is now in a much-diminished state. And the Catholic Church, which was then still wrestling with some of the outcomes from Vatican II, has now had to turn its attention to other challenges. It may seem, then, that this book's discussion of these theologies has little significance today.

It is important to see, though, that although some of the particular theological challenges to the gospel that we considered at the Hong Kong Consultation have diminished, the principles by which we engaged them have not. The reason, quite simply, is that these principles are biblical. Reading how these theologies were engaged brings to the fore the biblical truth by which they were engaged, and that endures for all generations.

The Base Line

Biblically speaking, the specifics of conversion, as we developed the theme in Hong Kong, will emerge in the pages that follow. Two central principles that are really nonnegotiable regarding Christian conversion is that first, Christian conversion is supernatural, and second, Christian conversion is unique. Unless it is both supernatural and unique in the ways in which we intend, conversion is not Christian. It is not real and it will not suffice.

Supernatural

In what sense is Christian conversion supernatural? There are, at the very least, three reasons for saying this. First, it is supernatural because without God's saving action in Christ, it would not be possible. Second, without the convincing work of the Holy Spirit, it would not seem desirable. Third, without the function of the inspired Scriptures in giving sinners the framework of truth in which to think, it would not be Christian. To these three reasons, the Reformed tradition has added a fourth: without the supernatural re-creative and regenerating work of the Holy Spirit, conversion would be impossible because regeneration and conversion are related as cause is to effect. This regenerative work of God, they argue, produces an overwhelming inward desire to turn from sin as well as the matching ability to believe in Christ. This divine work is what makes conversion possible. In this understanding, both repentance and faith are therefore the gifts of God, though it is the sinner who must turn from his or her sin and trust in Christ.

This account of Christian conversion, of course, is at odds with what is commonly understood outside the Christian world. For those outside of Christianity, conversion is understood in purely psychological terms and often as part of abnormal human behavior. They assume that changed behavior that results in a religious outlook can be explained by purely natural causes and often aberrant desires. Conversion in this understanding is self-originated and self-interpreting.

However, the biblical insistence is that conversion is neither self-originated nor self-interpreting. And this is true not only on the Reformed side of the equation. Historic Wesleyan Arminians agree that without the grace of God acting within a person's sinful disposition, there can be no passage to belief, no acceptance of the gospel. The difference is that historically Wesleyans have rejected the idea that this grace is an expression of God's choice in election whereas the Reformed affirm this. Yet, despite these differences, historic Wesleyans and the Reformed have united in seeing that Christ's substitutionary work is complete in and of itself: nothing can be added to it, nothing needs to be added to it, and nothing can be taken from it. It stands for all time and eternity, and it speaks decisively and permanently on behalf of those who seek the mercy and forgiveness of God.

And this is the proposition that must be grasped afresh in every generation, because there is within every sinner the deep impulse to resist the truth of their own helplessness and therefore to think that, even if full salvation is not within their grasp, they do at least make some contribution to their own redemption. It is as though God left our salvation incomplete and now waits for us as we complete what he left undone. This is the message that the Reformers opposed in the sixteenth century. Justification, without which there can be no conversion, does not need to be completed by our moral obedience, nor can it be, they contended, for then grace would not be grace. Today this same habit of wanting to insert at least a modicum of self-justification into our salvation has resurfaced. In the New Testament academy, the proponents of the New Perspective, Protestant though they may be, reiterate this argument, imagining that it is Paul's. And more widely, wherever evangelists and church marketers have diminished the doctrinal components of the gospel, there are those who fall back into ways of self-understanding that always seem to include belief in our ability to produce at least some aspects of self-justification.

The truth is that God's grace alone, grounded in Christ's objective work on the cross, accomplishes his redemptive purposes in us. Grace does not need to be completed by anything that we do, nor can it be. To say otherwise is to downgrade grace into mere divine influence, an influence that may or may not be effectual. But that is not grace as the Bible describes it, nor does it speak of the God of the Bible who, from first to last, has secured for us entirely what we could not do for ourselves, even in part. In this sense we must speak of our conversion as being supernatural even though it is we who must repent and believe.

Unique

Conversion, if judged by behavior, is not uniquely Christian; but Christian conversion, as we are understanding it here, is uniquely true. From the outside, a Christian's conversion may look like many other kinds of conversion. If, however, we understand that this conversion rests upon Christ, is grounded in him, looks to him, is supernaturally caused, and has eternal results, then it is unique as Christ himself is unique.

This truth has sometimes been inadvertently obscured in the evangelical world. This has often happened where biblical truth has lost its place in the church's thought and practice. Sometimes, though, this truth has also been obscured even where the formal authority of Scripture is recognized. An example is the way in which Christian testimonies have sometimes been used to advance the gospel. This is especially the case today, in the midst of the postmodern mood in which Westerners, at least, are living. In this climate, there is no overarching narrative to life. There are only our own small, petite narratives in which truth is what is true to the individual, not what can be true for everyone else. As a result, conversion stories are easily regarded as intensely private matters that are inscrutable to anyone else. Indeed, many outside of Christian faith, not least in the cults, also have their own "conversion" stories; so there is no way, nor any desire, to privilege one account over another.

If Christianity is true, and if conversion is a part of its message, then those who have turned to Christ will have a story to tell. They will have experienced God's forgiveness of sins. They will know what it is to return in the rags and tatters of human depravity, with no right to a place in God's house, and find the embrace of God. They will know what it is to be accepted by the Father, whose arms are opened wide, to be clothed in fine robes, and to take their seat at a welcoming banquet. They will experience the indwelling power of the Holy Spirit and will receive assurance of their salvation. If Christian faith is true—and it is!—there will be experience of which we can speak.

Nevertheless, we are not testifying to our own selves, as if our own personal biography had a compelling claim to everyone's attention. No, we are testifying to Christ! That, at least, is what witness-bearing in the New Testament is like. There, the focus is on the objective reality of God's redemptive work. It is to that reality, not to themselves, that early believers pointed. And this is what is unique; our experience is not. Indeed, human experience is hard to evaluate even for the person whose experience it is. How, then, are we to expect others who do not have a deep and accurate knowledge of our biography, who are not able to look within us and see our motivations, to be able to assess the credibility of our claims? People who give testimonies are usually strangers to us. How, then, can we discern authentic from inauthentic, true from counterfeit stories?

The truth of the gospel is not tied to our testimony to it. It is tied to what God did in Christ in reconciling us to himself. Therefore, while we can and should speak about our experience of this, that speaking needs to come in a framework that is also apologetic and draws people not to ourselves as those who are forgiven but to Christ through whom that forgiveness is found.

Additionally, the widespread use of testimonies, perhaps as a habit passed on from the revivals, has had the unintended consequence of placing an emphasis on conversion that the New Testament does not have. Undoubtedly, conversion is important, necessary, and indispensable to our being part of God's redeemed family. The point about conversion, though, is that it is the way into Christian faith; it is not the entirety of Christian faith. Conversion is only the threshold to the building of salvation. We are not called to stand, year in and year out, gazing at the threshold and testifying to it, but to enter the building.

Conversion does not stand alone; it is the beginning of a lifelong journey of growing in Christ and being conformed to his image. Discipleship must follow on conversion as living and breathing follow on birth. There is no life without birth and there is no Christian faith without regeneration and conversion. In the Christian world today, however, what we have all too often is an aberration—spiritual birth that is not followed by an obvious spiritual life. And that is what has produced considerable inauthenticity at the very moment when, in Western cultures, people are searching for what is genuine. They are looking for what is real amidst the hype and marketing frauds of modernity. Outside the context of personal authenticity, testimonies about being converted do far more harm than good.

Perhaps we can put this in terms of an older discussion. Today we insist that we must have Christ as Lord as well as Savior, which is an extraordinary admission of failure on our part. The apostles did not distinguish between having Christ as Savior and having him as Lord. For them, to receive Christ as Savior was to receive him as Lord at the same time. He could be had as Savior on no other terms. We have stood the New Testament on its head. We are often selling an anemic gospel that asks for little beyond the sales clinch and are then grateful for any who might adhere to it. Little is expected of them by way of moving beyond the threshold of belief and into a full-orbed discipleship.

Just as there is no discipleship without conversion, so there also can be no conversion without discipleship. The two belong together. That, at least, should be our insistence. And if we fail here, our testimonies to God's grace in our conversion become empty, discordant, and unbelievable.

Christian conversion, then, is unique not because we say it is, but because by its very nature it is. It is unique because it is grounded in the historical Jesus, who is identical with the risen Christ, and it is he who has objectively delivered us from sin, death, the devil, and God's judgment. Without this Christ there is neither faith nor conversion in any biblical sense. We turn from sin and we look in saving trust to Christ, uniquely God incarnate. Faith in such a Christ is as different from any other kind of "faith" as the Christ is different from any other object of trust.

The content that follows is arranged around an insight that is helpful today both in pastoral and evangelistic practice: the difference between insider and outsider conversions. To become a believer, a child of God, everyone must see Christ as their sin-bearer, must repent of their sin, and must in faith entrust themselves for time and eternity to him. Yet people come from different places to this point. Some have a long journey to make conceptually because the components of the worldview in which conversion belongs are not there. For others, these elements are there and so their journey toward this point of bowing before Christ is shorter. This is only making the point we know already, that in the New Testament, evangelism was not done in a "one-size-fits-all" mode, even if it is the same unchanging gospel to which all are called. In Acts, Paul varied his practice. In Acts 13:13–43, when he was speaking to Jews familiar with the Old Testament Scriptures, he could argue that Christ was their fulfillment. In Acts 17:16–34, when he was at Mars Hill and speaking to pagans, he made no reference to the Scriptures or to God's acts in history, but instead spent most of his time deconstructing their worldview, contrasting it with what is Christian. Only at the very end do we hear the first reference to sin in a veiled way—the first reference to Christ.

His approach with pagans was entirely different from his approach with Jews. This is a key insight not only in understanding New Testament practice but for our Christian practice today. Immigration has brought into our workplaces and neighborhoods many people from other parts of the world. Television and the internet have, in turn, made us citizens of the whole world. Its cultures, religions, and ethnic practices are now part of our consciousness. How important it is, then, to learn how to do what Paul modeled, which is to bring the truth of conversion to bear in the different contexts in which we so often find ourselves. These are the themes into which this book now leads us.

David F. Wells
August 2011

1

Christian Conversion

Christianity without conversion is no longer Christian, because conversion means turning to God. It involves forsaking sin, with its self-deifying attitudes and self-serving conduct, and turning to Christ, whose death on the cross is the basis for God's offer of mercy and forgiveness. Jesus was judged in our place so that God could extend his righteousness to us. Conversion occurs when we turn from our waywardness and accept Christ's death on our behalf. Without conversion, Christianity is no longer belief in Christ's substitutionary work, grace is no longer the unmerited and unalloyed action of God without whose work sinners die, and God is no longer the covenanting God whose purpose is to form a people for Christ as numerous as the stars (Eph. 2:11–22; Heb. 11:12).

When we turn to our traditional English Bibles, however, we discover that the word *conversion* appears only once, in the translation of Acts 15:3 (e.g., AV, RSV, NASB, NKJV), and a few times as a verb. Does this mean that we have made conversion a *sine qua non* of Christian faith when the Bible

does not? Is this a glaring instance of belief and practice aris-
ing at some later period in complete independence of—and
even in defiance of—what the Bible actually says?

This is a striking example of how misleading the study of
a single word can be! The Bible does teach the necessity of
conversion, but it uses different words to describe this process
and to emphasize its theological nature. The biblical writers
did not focus on the convert's feelings or emotions, but on the
content of the gospel. Thus the New Testament records several
dramatic conversion experiences (e.g., Paul, Acts 9:5ff.; Cornelius, Acts 10:44ff., cf. 15:7ff.; the Philippian jailer, 16:29ff.)
without showing any interest in the psychology of conversion.
Luke gives three accounts of the conversion of Paul (9:5ff.;
22:6ff.; 26:12ff.) and Cornelius (10:44ff.; 11:15ff.; 15:7ff.) because of the supreme importance of their conversions in early
church history, not to describe the manifestations that accompanied them. The New Testament writers view conversion
dynamically—as something one does—and they interpret
it theologically with words such as *faith*, *repentance*, *grace*,
forgiveness, and *regeneration*. We must examine these words
if we are to understand what conversion is and how it occurs.

Conversion encompasses both our behavior and what we
are in Christ. It primarily refers to repudiating sin and trusting in Christ, but this action does not stand alone. We repent
and believe that our sins might be forgiven and that we might
be given a new nature by the Holy Spirit to enable us to start
living a life of obedience and service to Christ. What we *are*
is theologically explained. What we *do* is a matter of our
behavior. A testimony should include both a description of
our actions (turning from our former life) and an explanation
of why we did so (Christ and his death for us).

The theological element (what we *are* in Christ) is the same
for every believer, including those who are near the faith when

28

they trust in Christ (e.g., the child raised in a Christian home, the Jew who believes in the truths of the Old Testament) and those who are far from the faith when they turn to the Lord (e.g., the skeptical atheist, the superficial materialist, the hard-edged Marxist ideologue, the bitterly opposed Muslim or Hindu, the enlightened Buddhist). The theological element of conversion is the same for people from the West and from the East, for the educated and the uneducated, for the young and the old, for those at the top of the social hierarchy and those at the bottom. The content of the gospel remains the same. It is the same Christ who has to be believed, for the same reason (the judgment of God upon sinners), in the same way (confessing our sinfulness and accepting God's provision in Christ), with the same result (hungering for his truth and righteousness, serving him in the world).

The difference in conversion stories lies not in what God has done for us in Christ but in *our* process of turning to him. A child raised in a Christian home may find conversion so natural that he or she cannot pinpoint when this change occurred. For others, however, the transition is difficult, conversion is dramatic, and the consequences in the community may jeopardize the convert's life.

In terms of the behavioral and psychological dimension, it might be helpful to distinguish between "insider" and "outsider" conversions. "Insider conversion" refers to people who have a substantial set of beliefs before coming to Christ; for example, Jews who believe in the Old Testament, children of Christian homes, churchgoers who accept the basic biblical truths but who lack a personal relationship with Christ. "Outsider conversion" refers to people who have little or no prior knowledge of Christianity and who may need to repudiate a large set of beliefs and practices before Christian conversion is possible. Such beliefs would include non-Christian religions, such as Hinduism, Islam, and Buddhism; alien ideologies, such as Marxism; and Western secularism, whose relativity and materialism constitute another form of idolatry.

The demarcation between insider and outsider conversion may not always be clear, but this is not significant. The purpose of this distinction is to reevaluate certain "models" of conversion experience that have been considered normative—specifically Paul's conversion. Certain evangelists try to reproduce a "Damascus road experience" in the lives of those to whom they preach. Some Christian parents look for dramatic "signs" of conversion in their children. If they fail to see such signs, they doubt the reality of their children's faith. The process of repenting and trusting is unique for every individual, because we have different expressions of sin and different worldviews. The theological explanation of conversion is the same. The behavioral components—what a person does to be in Christ—are affected by culture, personality, worldview, and prior lifestyle.

From God's perspective, all humanity is separated from him because of sin. As stubborn rebels bent upon the elevation of our selves and the repudiation of God and his truth, we are all far from God. Moral, religious people do not elude God's judgment—there is no alternative path, such as that proposed by the ecumenical, interreligious theology of the WCC. To be in sin is to be estranged from God, and that estrangement may be overcome only by belief in Christ's reconciling work. Spiritually speaking, there are only two categories: one is either saved or lost, a believer or a nonbeliever, in Christ's kingdom or in the kingdom of darkness.

From the sinner's perspective, however, some are nearer to the kingdom because they already believe in sin, the Trinity, and the divine nature of Christ. What they lack is an understanding that salvation is by grace through faith in the finished work of Christ who bore our sin on the cross and died in our stead. When such people take this final step, it gives vivid meaning to their earlier beliefs in God as triune, Christ as divine, and people as sinners. Their mental journey was short.

For others, the trip is quite long and involved. For an affluent, Western secularist to become a Christian, he or she must adopt Christianity's worldview, including its normative values, the ultimate distinction between right and wrong, a God who preserves that distinction in judgment, and a moral and spiritual order that is part of the fabric of everyday life. Such a secularist must jettison the idea that God is lost beyond the faraway cosmic background and that the self, with its felt needs and desires, is the fulcrum of life and its source of meaning. The secularist's mental outlook must be changed radically before he or she will be "close to the kingdom of God." The rapidity of conversion, however, cannot be equated with the length of the mental distance. Sometimes "insiders" are slow to take the final step in the conversion process, where outsiders readily jettison their old beliefs and practices. Both the distance and the speed involved in the journey of conversion may well affect the level of crisis and drama that attend the act of turning to and trusting in Christ.

We will begin by examining the biblical discussion of and language for conversion. Next we will consider the wider theological connections that the Bible makes.

Conversion

The Biblical Language

The Revised Standard Version and the New International Version of the Bible do not use any words from the Old Testament word group for conversion. The Hebrew verb *shubh* is the closest single-word equivalent for conversion in the Bible. *Shubh* is a common verb that usually is translated by the English "turn" or "return." It has a wide range of uses. *Shubh* is used one thousand times with no theological meaning. It is used over one hundred times to refer to spiritual relationship with God, particularly in the context of Israel's covenant with Yahweh.

In the Old Testament, individuals and the nation of Israel are called to "turn away" from evil or other gods and to "return" to God. The theme of Deuteronomy and of many of the prophets is that God's covenant people Israel are constantly liable to "turn away" from God (e.g., Jer. 2:27; 11:10) and so must be summoned to "return" to him (e.g., Hos. 6:1; 14:1).

Generally, *shubh* is used intransitively. Sometimes, however, it is used with an agent—either God (e.g., Ps. 80:3, 7, 14, 19) or someone else (prophets, Neh. 9:26; priests, Mal. 2:6)—who must return Israel to her true loyalty. Thus in the Old Testament there is a dual aspect to conversion: God "turns" people, and people "turn" to God. This is summed up by Jeremiah 31:18, which can be translated: "Turn me back and I will be turned," or, as Schniewind beautifully translates it, "Bring me home, then I shall go home."

This is "insider conversion"—the people of God are summoned to return to the covenant relationship that already exists. Even when they have been attracted to the worship of other gods, the presupposition appears to be that this is a temporary aberration—they are "really" God's people underneath. Thus the covenant context is crucial to an understanding of the significance of *shubh*.

Occasionally *shubh* is used in a noncovenantal context, as when the Ninevites "turn from" their wickedness even though they are outside of the covenant (Jon. 3:8, 10). Although the Old Testament holds out hope for the conversion of the Gentiles as the blessings of Abraham spread to "all the families of the earth" (Gen. 12:3), this hope is generally expressed in terms of Israel's special role as God's people. The Gentiles are to share in Israel's blessings, rather than turn to God in isolation. By the New Testament period, the hope for the inclusion of the Gentiles had developed naturally into a Jewish missionary concern to make proselytes—Gentiles who became Jews—insofar as this was possible.

Thus although *shubh* is the closest Hebrew equivalent to our term *conversion*, it is used in a covenantal, not an evangelistic, context in the Old Testament. *Shubh* does not focus on a decisive "change of religion" or on a personal, religious transformation through a once-only crisis. Instead, *shubh* emphasizes maintaining an existing covenant relationship through continual "turning" from evil to God, a process in which both God and the individual (or more typically the community as a whole) have a part. Josiah is characterized as one who "turned [*shubh*] to the LORD with all his heart and with all his soul and with all his might, according to all the law of Moses" (2 Kings 23:25) throughout his entire life. Josiah did not need a word to express conversion in our sense.

The New Testament usually uses *epistrephō* as an equivalent for the Old Testament *shubh*. Half of the thirty-six times *epistrephō* occurs it is used nonliterally and has a potential theological sense. Most of these uses occur in Luke's writings. Usually, *epistrephō* functions as an intransitive verb: people "turn" themselves (the only exceptions are Luke 1:16–17; James 5:19–20).

Several New Testament uses of *epistrephō* are derived directly from Old Testament uses of *shubh*.[1] In other cases *epistrephō* refers to a change in the life of a disciple: accepting

---

1. Matthew 13:15; Mark 4:12; Acts 28:27; John 12:40 use *strephō* instead of *epistrephō*, all quoting Isaiah 6:10; Luke 1:16–17 alludes to Malachi 4:6.

the revolutionary values of the kingdom of heaven (Matt. 18:3, using *strephō* rather than *epistrephō*), Peter's "return" after his failure (Luke 22:32), and a Christian's action in "bringing back" an erring fellow Christian (James 5:19–20). In its other New Testament occurrences, *epistrephō* refers to what we currently mean by *conversion*—non-Christians becoming Christians (with reference to Jews: Acts 3:19; 9:35; 2 Cor. 3:16; with reference to Gentiles: Acts 11:21; 14:15; 15:19; 26:18; 1 Thess. 1:9; in Acts 26:20 both Jews and Gentiles are explicitly mentioned). This same sense is clearly found in the one use of the noun *epistrephē* in Acts 15:3 to refer to "the conversion of the Gentiles." The use of the passive form of the verb in 1 Peter 2:25 probably has the same sense, though the situation from which the readers have "turned" is less specific.

Conversion, then, means returning or turning to God. Those within the Old Testament context needed a fresh understanding of what it meant to be a man or woman in covenant with God. Those outside of the covenant (today just as in biblical times) need to discover the filial relationship with God for which humanity was created, a relationship that was destroyed by sin but that is reestablished in the new covenant. Thus turning to God involves different things, depending on whether one turns as an outsider or as an insider.

Turning from the Outside

Three New Testament passages clearly illustrate the way *epistrephō* is used to refer to outsider conversion. The Thessalonians "turned to God from idols, to serve a living and true God" (1 Thess. 1:9). The Lycaonians were called to "turn from these vain things to a living God" (Acts 14:15). And Paul's mission to the Gentiles was "to open their eyes, that they may turn from darkness to light and from the power of Satan to God, that they may receive forgiveness of sins and a place among those who are sanctified by faith in me" (Acts 26:18). These passages highlight two distinct elements in conversion: conversion is *from* an old way of life and *to* a new and opposite allegiance. Both of these elements have their own New Testament vocabulary. The key word-groups are, respectively, *metanoeō* (repent) and *pisteuō* (believe). These words occur more frequently in the New Testament than *epistrephō* and are sometimes used together to denote the full "conversion process" (e.g., Mark 1:15; Acts 20:21). Repentance and belief go hand in hand—we cannot believe without repenting, and we repent in order to believe.

No one word captures all that becoming a Christian means, so it is not surprising that the various New Testament authors use an array of terms. Paul seldom uses *metanoia*, and John employs it only in Revelation. Paul often uses *pistis* (faith), and John employs the verb *pisteuō* (believe). The news about the Thessalonians' conversion from idols "to serve a living and true God" (1 Thess. 1:9) is summarized in the preceding verse as "your faith in God" (cf. Rom. 1:8 for a similar use). The members of Paul's churches are described simply as "those who believe" (1 Cor. 1:21; cf. Rom. 1:16), and Paul describes their coming to Christ as the time when "you believed" (1 Cor. 15:2, 11). John uses the same verb to describe the "conversion" of the Samaritans (John 4:39) and those Jews who became adherents of Jesus (e.g., 11:45, 48; 12:11, 42). He employs "believe in his name" as a virtual synonym for "receive Jesus" (1:12). Only those who "believe" will receive the blessings of salvation (e.g., 3:16; 11:25ff.).

The study of the three important word-groups (*epistrephō*, *metanoeō*, and *pisteuō*) only begins to reveal the New Testament language for conversion. The Holy Spirit's role at the beginning of conversion is vividly expressed as "being born again." This language is used not only by John (John 1:13; 3:3–8; 1 John 2:29; 3:9–10; 4:7; 5:4, 18) but also by Peter (1 Pet. 1:3, 23; 2:2), James (James 1:18), and Paul (Titus 3:5). Conversion also is expressed in terms of being resurrected with Christ into a new life (Rom. 6:3–4; Col. 3:1–4), putting off the old clothes and putting on the new (Gal. 3:27; Col. 3:9–10), a change of ownership (Rom. 6:17–18), moving from darkness into light (Acts 26:18; 2 Cor. 4:6; 1 Pet. 2:9; 1 John 2:9–11), and from death to life (John 5:24; Eph. 2:1–6).

To express an experience as transforming and supernatural as conversion demanded all the inventiveness of religious vocabulary. The overriding theme of transformation and newness is most forcefully summed up in Paul's crisp declaration in 2 Corinthians 5:17: "If anyone is in Christ, he is a new creation; the old has passed away, behold, the new has come"—all without using the word *conversion*!

In the case of Jewish evangelism, the line between insider and outsider conversion is necessarily blurred in the New Testament, the period during which Christian self-consciousness developed. It is inappropriate to ask at what stage the original disciples of Jesus "were converted" and to expect an answer in terms of our own expectations of conversion. No doubt God could tell us when Peter was "born again," but he has not done so. Only a bold person would try to fill the gap. If Peter had been a Greek, it might be easier to point to a specific time of conversion. As a Jew, Peter responded to a call from a Jewish prophet and only gradually understood that the call was more fundamental than a return to Old Testament covenant obedience.

The time at which conversion occurs is not always entirely clear, even in the cases of Gentiles in the New Testament, because some of them "became Jews" through proselyte conversion. Others remained outside of Judaism but accepted

36

its basic moral and religious values (Acts 10:1–4, 34–35). The time of Cornelius's conversion, however, seems clear: Peter spoke to him and his family, and "the Holy Spirit fell on all who heard the word" (Acts 11:44). Peter and his Jewish companions recognized this manifestation as the basis for baptizing them immediately as Christians. From Peter's perspective, this was outsider conversion and required the approval of the Jerusalem church (Acts 11:2–18). But from Cornelius's viewpoint, his conversion was not so much a radical break with the past as a "natural" progression of his religious experience. Socially speaking, Cornelius was indeed an outsider. But in terms of his religious status, though he was not a member of the covenant community, he already shared much of their practice and belief.

"Godfearing" Gentiles like Cornelius figure elsewhere in Acts, and some of them seem to have been similarly responsive to the gospel (Acts 16:14; 17:4; 18:7). Generally speaking, the "conversion of the Gentiles" (Acts 15:3) must have involved a more clear-cut transfer of religious affiliation, one that led to an immediately perceived change of life and loyalty. Peter, in particular, reported how some of the early Christians in Asia Minor (probably mostly Gentiles) found themselves alienated from their former associates by their Christian allegiance (esp. 1 Pet. 2:11–12; 3:13–17; 4:3–4, 14–16).

One of the great strengths of the gospel message is the way it breaks down community barriers, including those of race and religious affiliation. Paul often makes a point of this. According to Galatians 3:27–29, the basis of unity is "baptism into Christ." The old divisions listed in verse 28 are replaced not so much by a new creed as simply by "putting on Christ." This does not mean that Gentiles become Jews, for verse 28 eliminates that way of seeing things. Whatever their pedigree, in Christ all people are equally "Abraham's offspring" and share in the blessings of the people of God. Ephesians 2 makes the point even more strongly. Paul describes the Ephesians' former condition in Jewish terms—the "lost" condition of the Gentiles (vv. 1–3). But the grace of God not only gave them personal and heavenly salvation "in Christ Jesus" (vv. 4–10), it also broke down the community barrier and integrated the Gentile converts with Jewish believers as equal members of the household of God (vv. 11–21). From Israel's standpoint, Gentiles were "strangers to the covenants of promise, having no hope and without God in the world" (vv. 12–13). They were indeed outsiders, but "in Christ Jesus" all that has changed.

The ways in which insiders are approached with the gospel may be very different from the ways outsiders are approached. This is illustrated in the different preaching styles of Acts and in Paul's explanation in 1 Corinthians 9:19–23 of the different ways he witnessed to Jews and to Gentiles. The salvation offered is the same, and this salvation results in "one new man in place of the two" (Eph. 2:15), not in a community of Jews and another of converted Gentiles. This new community is "Abraham's offspring," the true fulfillment of the hopes and promises of Israel, though this does not make it a Jewish preserve. The old covenant boundary no longer applies; all have become insiders in Christ.

Thus insofar as there is a New Testament distinction between outsider and insider conversion, it is the person's sociological level and the degree of dislocation involved in joining the community of faith that distinguishes these two categories. There is no distinction at the theological level of what makes a true Christian and the new life and community that follow.

Turning from the Inside

The call to "repent" was the hallmark of John the Baptist's preaching and would have sounded familiar to any Jew who knew the Old Testament prophets. It is a classic use of *shubh*. John called Israel back to her true covenant allegiance, as the angel's announcement in Luke 1:16–17 indicated he would. John's ministry was a ministry to convert insiders—to turn the sons of Israel back to their God.

Jesus came as the Messiah of Israel to establish the reign of God through and among his people. His mission "to seek and to save the lost sons of Abraham" (Luke 19:9–10) was modeled on Ezekiel's vision of God's concern for the lost sheep of Israel.[2] Jesus did not call his Jewish hearers to join a new religion but to rediscover the relationship with God that should always have been theirs.

This is not to undervalue the radical transformation this must have brought in the lives of those who responded to Jesus's call. It was indeed a "conversion" they needed, but it was an insider conversion, the sort described in Matthew 18:3—accepting the status of children—a "turning around," or in our terms, a reorientation.

Even though this was not a "change of religion" in a sociological sense, the call to repentance, which was at the heart of Jesus's gospel (Mark 1:15), involved a radical change. This is illustrated by the twin parables of the treasure and the pearl (Matt. 13:44–46; cf. 2 Cor. 5:17). Paul describes this sort of reorientation in Philippians 3:4–11, where the noble values of the past are relegated to the status of garbage in comparison with the new values and aspirations found in Christ.

The radical discontinuity in the call to repentance and reorientation was graphically expressed in John's choice of baptism as the symbol of his converts' response. Although there is much debate over the possible antecedents of John's baptism, proselyte baptism probably was the only comparable

---

2. Ezekiel 34:1–16; cf. Matthew 10:5–6; 15:24 for this restriction in the mission both of Jesus and of his disciples.

39

rite known to his Jewish audience. When a Gentile wanted to become a Jew, he was baptized once to prepare him for his "new life." Before John's day, no one had proposed that Jews should be baptized in this once-for-all fashion. Anticipating their horrified reaction, John emphasized his point by noting that to be a "child of Abraham" was no guarantee of safety in the coming judgment. Only repentance that results in fruit could constitute such a guarantee (Matt. 3:8–10). Even Jews must be prepared to "start again"; the people of God need to be reborn.

The radical nature of repentance runs throughout Jesus's teaching and is reflected in his use of baptism to symbolize a new beginning. Jewish patriarchs will preside at a messianic banquet attended by "many from east and west," but Jews who expected to be there simply because they were Jews will be excluded (Matt. 8:11–12). A series of three devastating parables in Matthew 21:28–22:14 focuses on this theme of replacement. The Jews (pictured as the obedient son, the lawful tenants, and the invited guests) will find the tables turned: "the kingdom of God will be taken away from you and given to a nation producing the fruits of it" (Matt. 21:43). This is not to suggest that Gentiles will replace Israel or that Jews must become something else. The parables teach that Jewishness alone is not sufficient for salvation. The characteristic of the true people of God is not their genetic or community status but a fruitful relationship with God, a relationship now open to non-Jews. This same tension between Israel's continuity and discontinuity (the rejection of those who prove not to be "true Israel") runs throughout the New Testament. Paul summarizes this tension in his agonized discussion of the place of the Jews in Romans 9–11, with its illuminating allegory of the olive tree (Rom. 11:17–24). Some branches remain on the parent stock, others are grafted in from outside, but the tree remains "Israel." What determines the health of the branch is faith (v. 20).

Thus the gospel must be preached and salvation is available "to the Jew first and also to the Greek" (Rom. 1:16). The earliest Christian preaching (and almost the whole of Jesus's ministry) was a ministry to Jews that culminated in a call to repentance and a new beginning. In Acts 2:38 the formula is "Repent and be baptized in the name of Jesus Christ." Apparently those who responded were baptized immediately (2:41) as the mark of their membership in a new community (the followers of Jesus), even though that community continued to be seen as a part of Judaism. Converts continued to worship in the temple and to subject themselves to the disciplinary authority of the Sanhedrin. They viewed themselves as part of "Israel." When the question of admitting Gentile converts arose, it caused a long and bitter debate that was never finally resolved. In fact, it resulted in the separate existence of Ebionism, a conservative Jewish Christianity. For several centuries the Ebionite followers of Jesus saw themselves as the true culmination of Judaism, and Gentiles who wanted to convert had to become Jewish proselytes.

The definitive strand of Christianity arose from Peter's experience with Cornelius (Acts 10:1–11:18), the Gentile evangelism of the Christians in Antioch (Acts 11:20–26), and Paul's subsequent ministry to the Gentiles. The council of Jerusalem (Acts 15) accepted Paul's work and recognized Gentile followers of Jesus as members of the people of God in their own right who did not need to become Jews in order to be saved. Although Jesus's personal ministry deliberately focused on Jews, he clearly pointed forward to the redefinition of the people of God (e.g., Matt. 8:5–13; 28:18–20). The separate identity and self-consciousness of the new community grew until soon non-Christian Jews recognized it as a rival to their own community. By the mid-sixties, even the Roman emperor identified Christians as a distinct community. By about AD 85, the separation of Christians and Jews became so irrevocable that a "curse" on Christians and other heretics was included in the regular synagogue liturgy. Long before this date, the antagonism had developed to such an extent that John's readers found no difficulty in understanding his references to being "put out of the synagogue" because of loyalty to Jesus (John 9:22; 12:42; 16:2).

Thus what had begun as a movement calling for Jews to return to God (insider conversion) eventually demanded not only a new experience of God but also a change of religious affiliation (outsider conversion). This development was not due to any change in the nature of the gospel or to a change in the basis of a saving relationship with God. Both Christians and Jews recognized that a new community had come into existence, one that demanded a loyalty that was incompatible with continuing adherence to the parent group. Each claimed (no doubt with equal conviction) to be the "true" Israel, but their respective understanding of what that meant was now mutually exclusive. The symbolism already inherent in John's baptism—that Jews needed to be baptized to become "true Israel"—was now revealed in Christian baptism. For the Jew it marked a decisive break with the old community and entry into a new one.

The Wider Connections

Conversion and the Life of Convertedness

Whatever the route—whether from the inside or from the outside—conversion always means turning to Christ from unfaithfulness and sin to receive God's grace. After his resurrection, conversion occurs through God's Son, Jesus Christ.

For Jew and Gentile, insider and outsider, the same salvation is offered, received, celebrated, and proclaimed. This salvation results in the same responsibilities and demands the same obedience. Its beginning, center, and end is Christ.

However this relationship is initiated—quietly or dramatically, over a long or over a short period of time—it inaugurates a life devoted to serving God. Conversion is not an isolated event but is related to the entire life of faith that follows from it. It is the moment of birth into a new life. It is like a doorway into a room. A person is born to live, not to linger on the edge of the womb in a time limbo. A person opens a door not for the pleasure of standing forever on the threshold but to enter the room. The evangelical world has strangely perverted this truth. Evangelicals often make the test of spiritual life one's willingness to testify about the moment of birth. Describing one's sensations in passing through the doorway is considered proof that one is in the room! This shifts the focus from where it ought to be—the evidence of the Spirit's renewing work in producing a God-centered life, a God-fearing heart, and God-honoring character and witness—and places it on a person's autobiographical account of the conversion crisis. The only real proof of our conversion is an obedient and fruitful life.

This truth is most clearly taught in the parable of the sower and the seeds (Matt. 13:3–23; Mark 4:3–20; Luke 8:4–18), which was given at a time when enthusiasm for Jesus's teaching was growing and crowds were flocking to hear him. Evangelists do not usually discourage crowds, but Jesus told this and other parables to call those who had been born of God to himself (cf. 1 Pet. 1:23; 1 John 3:9). From an observer's (and apparently a participant's) point of view, there was initially no way of telling which soil would produce eternal fruit. At the behavioral level, three of the soils looked alike. The seeds sown on the rocky ground, among the weeds, and on the good soil all sprouted. In two of these locations, the germinating plants began to die, one as a result of shallow soil, the other because of the density of the surrounding weeds. One withered quickly, the other more slowly. Although these plants were doomed to perish, they sprang up just like the ones in the good soil that would endure and be fruitful. Initially the farmer did not know which was which. Only time would tell.

Unfortunately, some of the enduring lessons of the parable of the sower and the seeds have been forgotten from time to time. Often we regard enthusiasm or interest (like the appearance of a plant) as evidence of divine blessing. In actual fact, however, it may be nothing of the kind—the plant may be doomed to wither away. Religious enthusiasms are easily generated. Their reality is not measured by the degree of excitement they engender but by the quality of their endurance. The result of the test should be fruitfulness—the new character and the new direction of life that emerges. This is evident from the way conversion itself is treated in the New Testament.

This pattern is illustrated in the case of the woman taken in adultery. Those who teach this story sometimes forget to note Jesus's final phrase: "Go and sin no more" (John 8:11). Another example is Paul's pattern in the "no longer . . . but" passages: "[Christ] died for all, that those who live might live no longer for themselves but for him who for their sake died and was raised" (2 Cor. 5:15). Peter echoes this when he insists that a man should "live for the rest of his time in the flesh no longer by human passions but by the will of God" (1 Pet. 4:2). This passage reveals the antithesis that is the basis of the Christian concept of conversion. Conversion entails a denial of ungodliness and a life of sobriety, righteousness, and godliness (Titus 2:12), the avoidance of evil, and the conversion to God's will in thought and action. Christianity is inescapably preoccupied with changed lives.

Underlying this insistence is the apostolic understanding of conversion as a shift from following human instincts to obeying the divine will. As Jesus said: "I have come down from heaven, not to do my own will, but the will of him who sent me" (John 6:38; cf. 5:30). This is an exemplary passage for Christian ethics. Jesus also stated: "Whoever does the will of my Father in heaven is my brother, and sister, and mother" (Matt. 12:50). Christians are to seek first God's honor, not their own (John 7:18), and to seek Christ's interest above all self-interests (Phil. 2:21). Obedience to the first commandment is at stake. In short, conversion denotes a transformation from self-dedication to dedication to God.

First Peter 4:2 and the related passages primarily identify conversion as a change of will. "The lusts of man" and the "will of God" are both the volitional domain. Contrary to much of Greek and Western thought, this is the decisive realm for biblical thinking. Christianity is not merely interested in a change of being, worldview, or emotional deposition. Those called by God often deliberately disobey him (cf. Isa. 30:15; Matt. 23:37); thus the human will is the principal site of conversion.

The New Testament establishes the *moral nature* of conversion by calling for us to replace our desires with God's. The history of the human race is suspended between the antitheses of good and evil (Mark 3:4; John 5:28–29; 2 Cor. 5:10). In antithesis to any purely Gnostic understanding, Christian faith is "the way of righteousness" and a holy commandment delivered to believers (2 Pet. 2:21) by which they have been called to "depart from iniquity" (2 Tim. 2:19). The Old and New Testaments differ from much Greek thought because they understand truth morally, both as something that can be known and as that which must be done (1 John 1:6). The Bible teaches that truth can be suppressed by unrighteousness (Rom. 1:18), because it is essentially "truth according to godliness" (Titus 1:1). Therefore Paul emphasizes that Timothy had carefully followed not only his doctrine but also his conduct and aim in life (2 Tim. 3:10). Thus the goal of conversion is nothing less than loving God with all one's will, emotions, and thinking, whereas previously all of these faculties were engaged in self-love. Love grows from gratitude. It is the logical response of one who has been forgiven much (like the prodigal who begged to be made a hired servant but who was elevated and reinstated as a son of the house and made executive of its affairs [Luke 15:22]). Thus the love of God is the heart of Christianity toward which conversion must be directed. Although this may not always be understood, love of God (as Jesus indicates in John 5:42) is a sine qua non of Christian living.

According to Peter's teaching on conversion in 1 Peter 4:2, we should "no longer live . . . for the lusts of men, but for the will of God." The will of God is the double commandment of love, for God and for people. Conversion requires an honest examination of our past and of the practical steps we may need to take to make restitution for violations of our neighbor's interests. Zacchaeus's encounter with Jesus illustrates this (Luke 19:8). Thus conversion necessarily involves the restoration of human relationships.

Those converted through John the Baptist's preaching were charged to share their material possessions with others in need (Luke 3:11; cf. 1 Tim. 6:8). In his parable of the good Samaritan, which is a story about practical acts of caring—in this case for a man in immediate danger of losing his life (Luke 10:30ff.)—Jesus gives the authoritative interpretation of loving one's neighbor. Conversion leads to more than a life of religious exercises. It leads to deeds of benevolence and mercy. Conversion results in a religion that becomes socially tangible; it arrests the attention of all who claim to have the welfare of humanity in mind.

Above all, conversion implies a movement from theory to practice. God did not challenge his people in the Old Testament to "Be knowing, because I am knowing" or to "Be happy, because I am blissful." He charged them to "Be holy, for I am holy." It is essential "to observe my commandments and do them" (Lev. 26:3), just as God himself is "watching over my word to perform it" (Jer. 1:12). Correspondingly, John the Baptist cautioned his listeners: "Bear fruit that befits repentance" (Matt. 3:8). We cannot rely on religious pedigree and title. Jesus gave the same directions. He reminded the Jews that none of them kept the law (John 7:19; cf. Paul's similar argument in Rom. 2:13, 17ff.). He had no sympathy for the scribes and Pharisees, who "preach, but do not practice" (Matt. 23:3). It is essential to apply Jesus's teaching practically to our lives, not merely to pay lip service to it (Matt. 7:21, 24).

The key clause in the parable of the good Samaritan is not (as we might think) "to feel mercy" or "to show mercy" but "to do mercy" (Luke 10:37). Jesus tells those who understand this: "Go and do likewise." There is no element of religious fantasy, philosophical speculation, mere oratory, or ritual in the message and work of Jesus. His disciples understood this. They warned the church: "Let no one deceive you. He who does right is righteous, as he [Christ] is righteous" (1 John 3:7). "The kingdom of God does not consist in talk, but in power" (1 Cor. 4:20).

Christ captured the fundamental relevance of practicing righteousness in a short statement about distinguishing true and false prophets. One does not gather grapes from thorn bushes or figs from thistles (Matt. 7:16). Therefore the rule by which to measure prophets is "You will know them by their fruits" (Matt. 7:20). Jesus himself submitted to this rule: "These very works that I am doing, bear me witness that the Father has sent me" (John 5:36). Jesus insisted: "if I do not do the works of my Father, do not believe me. But if I do them, believe at least because of the works, if you do not want to believe me [as a person]" (John 10:37–38). But Jesus also applied this rule in his challenge to the Jews: "If you were Abraham's children, you would do what Abraham did" (John 8:39). It goes without saying that Christians themselves cannot hope to avoid the same rule: "He who says he abides in him [Christ] ought to walk in the same way in which he walked" (1 John 2:6; cf. 2 Tim. 2:19). Claim and conduct must be compatible.

Why is it so important that conversion not be limited to an inner experience but that restitution, moral uprightness, and providing for others also be evident? Why must the invisible renewal through the work of the Holy Spirit become visible in corresponding external expressions? According to the Bible, the Holy Spirit, though himself hidden and invisible, manifests himself in the lives and behavior of Christians (1 Cor. 12:7; cf. John 3:6–8). Thus it is necessary to manifest conversion through practical acts that become a testimony to other people and to the convert (cf. Matt. 5:16; 1 Pet. 2:12). The reality of conversion witnesses to God's lordship "in heaven above and on earth beneath" (Josh. 2:11; cf. the third petition of the Lord's Prayer, Matt. 6:10) and is not just a figment of metaphysics. In some ways, conversion is a testimony to the incarnation and humanity of God as the center of the Christian message.

One final reason for linking theory and practice (or faith and obedience) we might call the practical epistemology of the Christian religion. Obedience to what is already understood is the key to deeper insight. In other words, obedience is the key to knowledge. Concerning the mystery of his origin Jesus said: "If any man's will is to do his [God's] will, he shall know whether the teaching is from God or whether I am speaking on my own authority" (John 7:17). Who Christ is and what truth is cannot ultimately be decided at the level of theory and argument. Both are learned through practice and experience. In the same way, only those who expect to see a manifestation of God's glory are ready to answer the call: "Do whatever he tells you" (John 2:5).

Conversion and the Church

The seriousness with which conversion is regarded in the New Testament is revealed by the close relationship between conversion and baptism. In the accounts of group or individual conversion in Acts (three thousand on the day of Pentecost, Acts 2:41; Philip's converts in Samaria, 8:12; Simon, 8:13; the Ethiopian eunuch, 8:35–38; Cornelius, 10:44–48; Lydia, 16:14–15; the Philippian jailer, 16:31–34; Crispus, 18:8; Ephesian believers, 19:1–6) baptism is always specifically mentioned. In each case baptism occurred immediately after conversion. This suggests that baptism is intimately associated with the process of conversion as an outward ritual that symbolizes initiation into the Christian life.

In the evangelistic preaching in Acts, baptism is closely linked with the call to repent and believe the gospel. On the day of Pentecost, Peter preached to the crowds: "Repent and be baptized, every one of you, in the name of Jesus Christ for the forgiveness of your sins; and you shall receive the gift of the Holy Spirit" (Acts 2:38). Evangelism and the missionary call belong to the very nature of the gospel. Prior to his ascension, Jesus commissioned his disciples to "go therefore and make disciples of all nations, baptizing them in the name

49

of the Father and of the Son and of the Holy Spirit, teaching them to observe all that I have commanded you" (Matt. 28:19–20). In this spirit, Bishop Azariah (Dornakal, South India) used to ask those he was baptizing to put their hands on their heads and say with Paul: "Woe unto me if I preach not the gospel." Much modern evangelism omits the apostolic call to believe and be *baptized*.

Of course there is an obvious explanation for this. Evangelism today, especially mass evangelism, is usually not church-based. The evangelists minister apart from church connections and usually are unable to care for new converts. Furthermore, since baptism is an ordinance for churches to administer, it would be inappropriate for evangelists to begin baptizing randomly and promiscuously. The unintended result of this is that new converts are not put in touch with churches and so are left organically severed from the body of believers.

How very different is the New Testament situation! In the New Testament, converts were required to be baptized to make their allegiance to Christ public, even though this might result in ostracism or death. In the West today, baptism of children or of believers rarely is seen as a public proclamation of allegiance to Christ. But in Hindu and Islamic contexts it has this significance. In these societies Christian conversion is not seen as the ultimate offense against family and community, but Christian baptism is deeply offensive because it exposes a person's family, and even the community, to shame. Thus in the East, baptism is a painful and unavoidable test of the reality of a person's commitment to follow Christ. It reveals the depth and seriousness of the convert's intentions.

This discussion about baptism reminds us that the gospel not only initiates our relationship to God through Christ, but also calls us into organic fellowship with his people. Gospel preaching and pastoral care should never be separated.

Yahweh himself modeled this kind of pastoral care in his relationship to Israel. Israel was God's sheep, and he was their shepherd (Ps. 95:7). He was their Father, and they were his son (Hos. 11:1–4). How did this work out in practice? God's pastoral care is seen in his persistent calling, teaching, healing, leading, taking Israel in his arms, and easing Israel's yoke of slavery. Although God entrusted his sheep to undershepherds, such as prophets, priests, and kings, he gave them his Word, Spirit, and authority to accomplish their roles. And when they failed—often feeding themselves at the expense of the sheep, or ruling harshly and without regard for the truth—God repeatedly promised to send an entirely different shepherd through David's line (cf. Isa. 40:11; Jer. 23; Ezek. 34).

Christ came as the fulfillment of those promises. He was equipped with the Spirit to preach and to minister. He is the good Shepherd who laid down his life for his sheep. Jesus's identification with sinners is a model of pastoral care (Luke 15:1–2; 19:1–10; John 4:1–42). He was sensitive to physical needs such as hunger (Matt. 15:32–39; John 21:9–14). He restored the despised (like Zacchaeus in Luke 19:1–10). He pitied the diseased (Luke 9:2; 10:9; John 5:1–9). He was patient with those who learned slowly (Matt. 15:5–12; John 20:26–29). He was concerned for backsliders (Luke 22:31–32; John 21:15–19) and for those who were spiritually hungry (Mark 6:34; Luke 5:1–3). He prayed for his own (Mark 1:35; Luke 22:31–32; John 17:1–26). After his resurrection he charged his apostles and the church to extend this care to others by teaching, shepherding, and supporting—by doing anything necessary to make disciples out of sinners. This type of care still needs to be extended to converts so that they may see the life and love of Christ exemplified in the Christian community. Where their families have rejected them, they need to find acceptance. Where they have physical need, they should find relief. Where they have doubts, they should find teaching and care. Where they need to be undergirded and strengthened, they should find support as Christ works through his people. Jesus died not only to offer forgiveness but also so that we might become free from sin. This lifelong process cannot be accomplished without the church.

In this chapter, then, we have seen that all Christians have the same basic type of relationship to God through Christ. This relationship is foreshadowed in the Old Testament by Abraham's relationship with God through faith. The Christian's relationship with God is established on and by God's grace, which required Christ to take our sin on himself and to give us his righteousness. God's grace is received by faith, and it results in forgiveness and a new nature. Our relationship with God is established by God. All who know him know the same God, by the same Christ, through the same Holy Spirit, and as a result they belong to one body or family. How people come to this knowledge differs with culture, life experience, personality, and worldview.

We have distinguished between insider and outsider conversion, between those who bring much and those who bring little basic belief to their encounter with the gospel. This distinction may help us understand different experiences of conversion, and it should make us more cautious about standardizing a particular form of crisis experience as a normative way of defining conversion. We will look at this aspect of conversion in more detail in the next chapter.

2

Insiders

Insiders. The word has bad connotations! It can refer to persons who use privileged knowledge for their own advantage—such as stock market brokers who profit by trading on insider information—or to business tycoons, political moguls, and the social elite. By definition, outsiders are excluded from what insiders consider important. But we are not using *insiders* in any of those senses.

We are using *insiders* in a theological sense to refer to those people who already understand and believe a substantial amount of what the Bible teaches when they hear the gospel. We need to understand how conversion occurs for them. In later chapters we will look at the same subject in terms of outsiders: Muslims, Hindus, Buddhists, and Marxists. In this chapter we will focus on the life and conversion of Paul, and, as an interesting counterpart, on the conversion of children.

Paul

If we are to understand the biblical concept of conversion, the best place to begin is with the conversion of Paul. Paul's conversion stands out dramatically in the New Testament, and it has influenced the church's understanding of conversion more than that of any other individual.

Paul's conversion was unusual in at least three senses. Paul was an insider, his conversion was dramatic, and it resulted in his commission as the apostle to the Gentiles. How normative, then, is Paul's experience? To what extent and in what ways can it serve as a model of Christian conversion? Should we always expect and perhaps try to produce the same elements of drama and crisis that Paul experienced? To answer these questions, we must carefully examine the biblical record.

The Account of Paul's Conversion

In Acts, Luke emphasizes important events by devoting more space to them (e.g., Pentecost, Stephen's witness) or by describing them several times (e.g., Peter's visit to Cornelius—Acts 10 and 11). In the case of Paul's conversion, Luke used both techniques to draw attention to the theological importance of this event. Luke described Paul's conversion three times (Acts 9:1–9; 22:3–21; 26:4–20), devoting a considerable amount of space to it.

These three descriptions are not identical. The variations between the accounts may be explained in terms of different narrative forms and dissimilar historical circumstances. In Acts 9 the account of Paul's conversion forms part of Luke's explanation of how the gospel spread from Jerusalem to the Gentile world. In Acts 22, before an angry Jewish crowd in Jerusalem, Paul explained his missionary call by describing his conversion. In Acts 26 at his trial before Agrippa, Paul's explanation of his conversion formed part of his defense. The demands of each situation account for the differences between the records. For example, in Acts 22:12 it was relevant to describe Ananias as a "devout man according to the law, well spoken of by all the Jews." Despite such differences, the major features of Paul's conversion are clear in all three accounts. Paul completely changed his attitude toward Jesus and his followers. He wanted to obey Jesus as Lord, and he was called to take Jesus's name before the Gentiles. In all three conversion narratives, there is an implicit or explicit sense of new life and forgiveness of past sins. Two of the three accounts mention baptism.

In Paul's epistles the most significant passages on his conversion are 1 Corinthians 15:8–10; Galatians 1:13–17; and Philippians 3:4–14. In the Corinthian passage, Paul states that the risen Christ appeared to him and called him to be an apostle, even though he had persecuted the church of God. Perhaps it is appropriate to read 1 Corinthians 15:8–10 in the light of 2 Corinthians 4:6, which says: "For it is the God who said, 'Let light shine out of darkness,' who has shone in our hearts to give the light of the knowledge of the glory of God in the face of Christ."

Paul's description in Galatians 1 of his conversion is similar to that in 1 Corinthians 15:8–10. In Galatians 1 Paul said that God "was pleased to reveal his Son" "in" or "to" him (the Greek preposition *en* implies that an inward experience accompanied external phenomena). Paul's conversion involved a "calling" and a "setting apart" that he "might preach him [Christ] among the Gentiles" (Gal. 1:16).

Philippians 3:4–14 does not allude to the moment of Paul's conversion but to the transformation of his life. Because of his conversion, Paul, the former persecutor, counted all that he had once deemed gainful "as loss for the sake of Christ" (Phil. 3:7). After his conversion, Paul's mind was filled with "the surpassing worth of knowing Christ Jesus my Lord" (Phil. 3:8). The account in Philippians of Paul's conversion specifically mentions what is only implicit in 1 Corinthians

15:8–10 and Galatians 1:13–17—turning from dependence on "righteousness under the law" to "that which is through faith in Christ, the righteousness from God that depends on faith" (Phil. 3:9).

Thus there are no significant differences between the three accounts of Paul's conversion in Acts and Paul's description of his conversion in his epistles, where he explains its theological significance. We need to examine the substance of Paul's conversion in more detail by looking at its biographical and theological aspects.

The Shape of Paul's Conversion

Paul's conversion was not a simple event. It was a multifaceted experience. To understand it properly, we must examine its various facets.

What did it mean for Paul to be converted? Many things! Instead of opposing Christ, Paul submitted to him. Instead of being alienated from God, Paul was reconciled to him. Instead of being spiritually dead, Paul was spiritually alive by means of the Spirit. Instead of assaulting Christians, Paul joined them. Before his conversion Paul had not looked beyond Israel. After his conversion Paul took the gospel to the Gentiles. We need to explore each of these aspects of Paul's transformation.

First, conversion for Paul meant turning to Christ in submission and yielding to his service. The persecutor of Christ became his protagonist. Both Acts and the Pauline epistles portray Saul before his conversion as one who "persecuted the church . . . and tried to destroy it" (Gal. 1:13). Such statements indicate that Paul had some knowledge of the Jesus whom the church proclaimed. Paul was present at Stephen's trial, defense, and stoning. Therefore Paul must have known the claims that Christians made for Jesus: the crucified one had been raised from the dead and thus shown to be "both Lord and Christ" (Acts 2:36). Since Paul tried to arrest Christians wherever possible, he could not have been ignorant of Jesus's trial before Caiaphas or of his response when challenged: "Are you the Christ, the Son of the Blessed?" (Mark 14:61). Saul was determined to stamp out belief in Jesus as "Lord" and as "Son of God" by denying Jesus's resurrection and his identity as the Christ.

On the road to Damascus, however, Jesus "made me [Paul] his own" (Phil. 3:12) in a way that caused Paul to compare his experience of the risen Lord with the experience of those who saw the risen Lord before his ascension. According to Paul, "Last of all, as to one untimely born, he appeared also to me" (1 Cor. 15:8). Elsewhere Paul asked: "Have I not seen Jesus our Lord?" (1 Cor. 9:1). In Acts this is described as a light that blinded him. Galatians 1:12 refers to it as "a revelation of Jesus Christ." Saul could no longer doubt that the crucified Jesus was risen, and he was prepared to submit to him. "What shall I do, Lord?" Paul asked (Acts 22:10). Soon after submitting to Jesus as the risen Lord, Paul began to bear witness to him as the "Son of God" and the "Christ" (Acts 9:20, 22). Paul's conversion involved turning to Jesus and coming to know and acknowledge him as the living Lord.

Second, Paul's conversion resulted in his justification, acceptance, and forgiveness. According to his own testimony and that of others, Saul's early life was marked by an intense moral earnestness. "I advanced in Judaism beyond many of my own age among my people, so extremely zealous was I for the traditions of my fathers" (Gal. 1:14). Paul described his life as a Pharisee in this way: "As to the righteousness under the law, blameless" (Phil. 3:5). But Paul's belief in self-righteousness was shattered by his conversion. Philippians 3 shows that Paul's conversion completely changed his view about how to gain God's acceptance and how to be counted righteous. Paul's post-conversion understanding was that "righteousness . . . is through faith in Christ, the righteousness from God that depends on faith" (Phil. 3:9).

In Philippians 3:9 Paul describes his new standing before God without explaining how it came about. In Galatians and Romans, Paul attributes it to Jesus's death on the cross. "This righteousness from God," he says, "comes through faith in Jesus Christ" (Rom. 3:22 NIV). Those who believe "are justified freely by his grace through the redemption that came by Christ Jesus. God presented him as a sacrifice of atonement" (Rom. 3:24–25 NIV).

How soon after his conversion and by what stages Paul came to this understanding we may not be able to say, but it represented a complete repudiation of his former understanding of Jesus's crucifixion. As one brought up in the law and traditions of Israel, Paul believed that a crucified person was accursed (Gal. 3:13, quoting Deut. 21:23). Thus the message of a crucified Christ was inevitably "a stumbling block [Greek *skandalon*] to Jews" (1 Cor. 1:23; cf. Gal. 5:11). But this message became Paul's greatest joy; nothing else mattered (1 Cor. 2:2). Because Jesus bore our sin on the cross, he opened the way to righteousness, justification, acceptance with God, and forgiveness. Paul received the heart of his gospel—its basic principles—"through a revelation of Jesus Christ" (Gal. 1:12) on the Damascus road. Paul's turning to Christ meant turning to God in a new way: in dependence on God's grace, not in dependence on his own lawkeeping.

Third, Paul attributed his conversion to the work of the Holy Spirit, who gives life to the dead. Although Paul's description of God's role in turning a person to Christ may have developed later, immediately after his conversion Paul was conscious of having received a new life through God's Spirit, a life that resulted in completely transformed behavior. In Acts 9:17 Ananias laid hands on Saul not only to restore his sight but also so that he would "be filled with the Holy Spirit." In 2 Corinthians 5:17 Paul says: "If anyone is in Christ, he is a new creation; the old has passed away, behold, the new has come." This is the fruit of "reconciliation" to God. Paul describes his old way of life as gone, dead and buried, as symbolized by baptism (Rom. 6:1–4). "I have been crucified with Christ; it is no longer I who live, but Christ who lives in me; and the life I now live in the flesh I live by faith in the Son of God, who loved me and gave himself for me" (Gal. 2:20). Paul refers to this new condition as "Christ in him," as being "in Christ," as being "in the Spirit," and as having "the Spirit of God dwelling in him" (Rom. 8:9). Paul rings the changes on these words and images, all of which refer to turning from life "according to the flesh" to life "according to the Spirit" (Rom. 8:4), from law to grace, from death to life, from darkness to light, and from loss to gain. Through the Holy Spirit, God makes all of these changes possible.

Although Paul's metaphors imply a once-for-all experience, they also indicate continuing change. Baptism identifies us with Christ's death and resurrection. It symbolizes a decisive death to the old life and an equally definitive reception of new life. Nevertheless, Paul also said: "I die every day!" (1 Cor. 15:31; cf. 2 Cor. 4:10–12). Even at the time of his conversion, Paul needed to realize "how much he must suffer" for the sake of Christ (Acts 9:16).

Fourth, Paul's conversion immediately affected his persecution of Christians. Although his conversion was a deeply personal and individual experience, it led Paul to associate with the very people he had tried to destroy. In the first words of the "heavenly vision," Jesus informed Saul that persecuting his disciples meant opposing and persecuting him. Thus turning to Christ means identifying with his followers. Immediately after recovering his sight and being baptized, Paul "was with the disciples of Damascus" (Acts 9:19). In Galatians 1 Paul had his reasons for asserting his independence from the Jerusalem apostles, but this did not mean that he was a solitary disciple. His fellowship with the church in Jerusalem and in Damascus—and anywhere else—was clearly vital to him (Acts 9:26–29; Gal. 2:1–10).

Finally, in the three accounts in Acts and in the account in Galatians 1, Paul's conversion is inseparably linked with his call to be the apostle to the Gentiles. In Acts 9:15 the Lord tells Ananias: "He is a chosen instrument of mine to carry my name before the Gentiles and kings and the sons of Israel." Christ told Saul: "I send you [to the Gentiles] to open their eyes, that they may turn from darkness to light and from the power of Satan to the power of God, that they may receive forgiveness of sins and a place among those who are sanctified by faith in me" (Acts 26:17–18). The form of Paul's calling to be the apostle to the Gentiles is expressed in various ways in Acts 9, 22, and 26, but in each case it is inseparably linked with the conversion narrative. More significantly still, Paul himself says that God's purpose in revealing Christ to him was "in order that I might preach him to the Gentiles" (Gal. 1:16). More simply and tersely, Paul declares that through Jesus Christ "we have received grace and apostleship" (Rom. 1:5). The grace of Paul's coming to be "in Christ" was inescapably associated with his call to be an apostle—"to bring about the obedience of faith for the sake of his name among all nations" (Rom. 1:5).

It is difficult to say how suddenly or by what stages Paul realized the implication of the revelation he received on the road to Damascus, a revelation that constrained him to preach the gospel (1 Cor. 9:16; 2 Cor. 5:14) and to make Christ known wherever he was not known before (Rom. 15:20). During the three days he was blind, Paul may have come to a new understanding of Scripture based on his "heavenly vision." It is still a matter of debate whether Paul's "going away into Arabia" (Gal. 1:17) was to meditate on the implications of his sudden conversion or for evangelism. Although Paul's understanding of the relation between his call to apostleship and his mission to the Gentiles may have developed over time, the New Testament documents indicate that Paul's conversion to Christ resulted in a commitment to evangelize the world.

These elements of Paul's conversion are inextricably part of his experience. They were the ground for, the means of, and the consequence of believing God. But Paul was converted as an insider. Now we will see how the Spirit may have prepared Paul for his encounter with Christ on the Damascus road.

A good place to begin is with Jesus's words to Paul: "it hurts you to kick against the goads" (Acts 26:14). These words portray an ox that kicks at the ploughman but hits only the plough, thus hurting itself in vain. To his own detriment, Paul tried to oppose Jesus Christ with all the energy he could summon. Truth and reality were the goads that Saul resisted, but God used them to convince Paul of the right way. Perhaps the process of Paul's conviction began when he witnessed Stephen die a martyr's death at peace with God (Acts 7:58; 22:20).

Paul was earnestly committed to pursuing righteousness through lawkeeping. Had he begun to wonder whether he had failed to win acceptance with God on this basis? There is understandable debate regarding how far Romans 7 is auto-biographical, but it could hardly be totally unrelated to Paul's own experience. Romans 7 is especially significant because Paul says he came to know sin through the particular law "You shall not covet" (Rom. 7:7). Even before his conversion, did Paul realize that at least one of the commandments had to be kept not only in word and deed but also in the very thoughts of the heart? And did this realization also result in a kicking against God's goads?

The Spirit of God may have prepared Paul in other ways for his call as apostle to the Gentiles by convincing him that God's plan for him was contrary to the path he so earnestly pursued. Saul was brought up at the feet of Gamaliel (Acts 22:3) as a rabbinic scholar (Gal. 1:14), a strict Pharisee (Acts 26:5), and a "Hebrew born of Hebrews" (Phil. 3:5). He was also a man of Tarsus and a Roman citizen, and as such he must have imbibed something of the expansiveness of Greek culture and the spirit of the mighty Roman Empire. Could Jewish exclusiveness be right in the light of the prophets' vision of the knowledge of the living God of Israel spreading to all nations? Perhaps it is speculative to suggest it, but could Paul have wondered whether there was another way to fulfill the hopes and prophecies of Scripture? Perhaps such a fulfillment was to be found in a spiritual reality that transcended law and temple, the sort of reality envisioned by the followers of Jesus and described by Stephen.

Let us speculate a bit more. There are many ways in which questions could have arisen in Saul's mind, perhaps through the warning words of Gamaliel (Acts 5:34–39) or by some knowledge of the earthly life of Jesus (2 Cor. 5:16). Whatever the details, divine election (Acts 9:15; Gal. 1:15) and the divine initiative of God's Spirit were at work in Paul's circumstances, heart, and conscience. They were also at work in his mind, which was steeped in the Old Testament Scriptures, nurtured on their truth, and vulnerable to the exposure of their light. When the time came, Paul no longer kicked against the goads but submitted himself to the Lord of glory.

Now we are in a position to ask ourselves what was normative about Paul's conversion. What aspects of Paul's biography should be true of all Christian conversions? Immediately we can discount three elements. First, we do not need to come to Christ as Jews, for Paul himself was sent to preach the gospel to the Gentiles. Second, we cannot be commissioned to be apostles as Paul was, because the social qualifications needed for this office can no longer be met. The office of the apostle ceased when the last of the New Testament apostles died. Thus the link between Paul's conversion and his calling to be an apostle are not normative. Third, Christ need not appear audibly and visibly to us for a genuine conversion experience to occur. This is verified by the many lives that were changed as a result of Paul's preaching.

What, then, are we to make of Paul's experience with Christ on the Damascus road? Is it normative? The answer from Paul's writings is that it is normative theologically but not experientially. In Galatians 1 and Philippians 3, when Paul spoke of the transformation of his life, he did not draw attention to the blinding light or to his ecstatic experience. The encounter and its drama and crisis are not important. What is important is the change that took place in Paul's life and the theological interpretation of that change.

What is normative in Paul's conversion is submission to the same Christ he met, not the "Christ" of modern theology (who is not defined by the historical Jesus) or the "Christ" supposedly concealed in non-Christian religions. We submit to the divine-human Christ who is revealed in the Bible and in whose life, death, and resurrection we find God's unique, saving self-disclosure. God's self-disclosure in Christ is gracious, because God reveals himself to those who have no claim upon him, to those who in their rebellion have opposed and excluded him. God pardons us through Christ's death in our place. As Paul learned, the gospel is not a word about our self-effort but about God's mighty acts in Christ on our behalf. Striving toward God, inside or outside of his law, can never be the basis of acceptance with him. If acceptance on that basis were possible, Christ's death would have been unnecessary. In being found by Christ, we are led from our old way of life, with its sin and spiritual death, into a new way of life that is characterized by righteousness and eternal life. Being in Christ must result in a life where his truth, purity, and love are seen. It also will inevitably result in suffering and rejection. Being in Christ also will mean that we will be drawn irresistibly to his people, and with them we will serve Christ by making his gospel known to the world. These elements in Paul's conversion are normative and indispensable for us today. It is in these ways that Paul was an outstanding example of how the grace of God reaches out to sinners (1 Tim. 1:15–16).

Children

Some might question the propriety and validity of juxtaposing Paul's conversion and the conversion of children. Why should children be included as insiders? Certainly this comparison could be misleading. Some present-day evangelicals have portrayed elements of Paul's conversion as normative that Paul did not deem normative; for example, the suddenness, crisis, and drama of the event. In some evangelical circles, these are understood as hallmarks of a "genuine" conversion. Consequently, evangelicals often evangelize children in a way designed to bring them to a point of "decision."

The children of Christian parents, however, sometimes do not have extended, clearly defined periods of rebellion they can remember and against which they can contrast their conversion. A child from a Christian home does not always clearly remember when he or she crossed the line from unbelief to belief. Even for children outside a Christian family, conversion may be more like a transition or a growth into Christ than a sudden and abrupt about-face like Paul's. Unless this is recognized, both evangelists and children will use the wrong criteria to measure conversion. They will look for suddenness, crisis, and drama, and if they do not find them, they may conclude that a genuine commitment to Christ has not occurred. Indeed, people who work with children have often encountered those who have made multiple "decisions for Christ" and who are still quite uncertain about their relationship with God.

The center of the Christian faith is a relationship with God through Jesus Christ that is based on understanding and believing the gospel. The element of understanding has been the focus of considerable discussion. What can children know and how much must they know before conversion can occur? In *Religious Thinking from Childhood to Adolescence* (1964), Ronald Goldman warned about certain dangers in the evangelism of children. Some who evangelize children impose too much formal Bible knowledge at too early an age on children who are not capable of assimilating such knowledge. The current understanding of how children think is fluid; many of the older Piagetian assumptions are being challenged.

For many children, including those outside of Christian families, the first emphasis should be on a relationship with God. For others, what they know in theory will be experienced in relationships. Children are capable of belief, but as they experience new stages of life and personal development, their level of understanding (and belief) needs to grow. For children from Christian and non-Christian homes, this development will be characterized by many decisions toward Christ before the line is actually crossed into his kingdom.

These decisions include the acknowledgment of Christian teaching, a growing awareness of personal sinfulness, and a desire to be right with God. For this reason, children (even those from non-Christian homes) often move toward Christ more like insiders than like outsiders.

Only God knows the exact moment of conversion for any person, including children. The evangelist's responsibility is not to create or demand a predetermined response but to teach about the gospel, so that the child continues to respond until he or she reaches the point of trusting in Christ and the benefits of his death and resurrection. The point of comparison with Paul is not the experiential aspects of the Damascus road conversion (Paul himself did not consider his experience normative); it lies elsewhere.

First, like Paul every child is a sinner who needs to be forgiven on the basis of Christ's work. With submission to Christ comes the Spirit's supernatural work of new birth and his reorientation of the sinner to Christ's values and service. Second, because the child is immature and is in the process of developing, conversion is often preceded by incremental movements toward Christ rather than by a sudden shift in worldview, such as might occur for an adult outsider. Therefore evangelists should exercise great sensitivity as they enter into the child's world—a world of immaturity but not necessarily of innocence. Today's children often have been exposed to or know about violence, brutality, and abuse at increasingly younger ages. Their childhoods are disappearing. Competitive, affluence-oriented interests intrude very early into their experience. Wars and calamities also may shape their outlook. It requires sensitivity and empathy to help a child move toward and into a relationship with Christ.

Our failure or neglect to reach children with the gospel might seem unimportant today, but in the future it will loom larger and larger. After all, in the ranks of today's children are tomorrow's world, national, and community leaders—the future philosophers, poets, theologians, scientists, doctors, politicians, preachers, counselors, and parents who will shape the basic values of their children. A life directed toward Christ at an early age can have enormous impact on the family and the world. The reorientation of values and worldview associated with Christian conversion could revolutionize the future of individuals who will shape tomorrow's world.

In this chapter, then, we have considered in some detail the most famous of all Christian conversions, that of Paul, and in less detail the conversions of children. The point in linking them together in a single chapter is the opposite of what might appear to be the case. It may seem that the intention is to establish as a model for the conversion of children the circumstances of drama and crisis that attended Paul's conversion. Evangelists have, in fact, often done this. This chapter has argued the reverse of that. It is *not* the drama and crisis of his conversion that Paul considered normative, for children or anyone else, although like Paul, some may experience dramatic conversions that are attended by a painful sense of crisis. Paul's focus in telling about his own conversion was theological and not psychological.

The point of comparison between Paul and children, then, is theological and, specifically, that children are in the pattern of insider conversion. Paul and children are, however, insiders for different reasons. Paul's conversion fell into this pattern because of what he already knew: his profound knowledge of the Old Testament Scriptures, his training in Judaism, his zealous acceptance of many of the truths without which there can be no gospel. Paul already believed in the one God, accepted biblical revelation, understood its teaching on sin and the need for sacrifice, believed in God's judgment, and in some way anticipated a Messiah. This was not a small foundation upon which the gospel could rest! For children the pattern of coming to Christ is similar, not because they bring with them this set of beliefs, but because they need to have them built up as a preparation for the gospel. They need to come into saving faith by incremental stages, making steps toward Christ as their knowledge of biblical truth grows and as their awareness of themselves as sinners increases. It is important to build this foundation with patience and care and to resist the temptation to produce instant conversions. Young children often want to please parents and adults and it is therefore not difficult for teachers and evangelists to manipulate them into making a decision. But even if this is done with the best of motives, it is not the best, or even a desired, result. For what results is a misunderstood experience that later on may rebound in the form of a bitter resentment and disillusionment.

What is important is that the gospel be given a context, that it be understood within the framework that the Bible itself gives to it, that it be seen to grow out of God's holiness and love, that it be understood as addressing people, not simply for them to make a decision, but for them to understand their plight before God as defiant sinners. The gospel has no staying power, in the lives of adults or children, if it is torn from these connections. Then it becomes simply one more commodity for sale in a world flooded with competing commodities. Children not only can understand such matters, they must understand them. And it is a mark of wisdom on our part if we are willing to give them time to build these connections rather than short-circuiting the process in the interests of having conversion "results."

3

How and Why We Turn

Conversion can be spoken of as a single act of turning, just as consuming several dishes and drinks can be spoken of as a single act of drinking. A significant part of the evangelical world encourages us to think of a simple, all-embracing, momentary crisis as the standard form of conversion. But conversion, our turning to God, is better understood if we view it as a complex process. The process involves thinking and rethinking, doubting and overcoming doubts, soul-searching and self-admonition, struggle against feelings of guilt and shame, and concern as to what a realistic following of Christ might mean, whether or not it culminates in a personal crisis that will afterward be remembered as "the hour I first believed." Sometimes, of course, it does so culminate, outside as well as inside revivalist circles; think of Augustine hearing a child say "take and read," picking up a Bible and seeing Romans 13:13, and never being the same again. But sometimes the process does not climax in a single conscious crisis, even for those who attend evangelistic crusades. God is Lord in conversion, as elsewhere, and our experiences of his dealings with us differ.

Some decisions that occur within the structural pattern of revivalist evangelism are preceded by little of this soul-travail. As we know, many of these decisions prove hollow, and if 10 percent of the professed converts in a crusade are still faithful after a year, evangelists and pastors pronounce it a great success. What is touted in the press—the victory that is so easily declared—obscures the spiritual depression and confusion that are also sown. What happens to the substantial number of people who "decide" for Christ but find that their decision was apparently empty of spiritual reality? And who is to accept the responsibility for this situation—the person who made the decision or the person who elicited it? We would be wise to consider this matter more carefully than we have in the past.

It is already apparent that what we may look for, or think has taken place, in a "decision for Christ" is complex. It is therefore helpful to begin by distinguishing what is objective in it from what is subjective. The objective means of conversion is the gospel message, opened by the Spirit to the spiritual eyes as part of his renewal of our hearts. "Faith comes from what is heard, and what is heard comes by the preaching of Christ" (Rom. 10:17); "Of his own will he brought us forth by the word of truth" (James 1:18); "Believe in the Lord Jesus, and you will be saved" (Acts 16:31). The message is twofold: law and promise, law and love, law and grace. "Law" stands for God's demands, our failure to meet them, God's declared judgment, our need of a reconciled relationship with him, and our misery without that relationship. "Promise, love, grace" stand for announcing Christ, the divine Savior, crucified, risen, and reigning, living, forgiving, and befriending; for inviting sinners to come to him and through him to the

Father; and for setting all that within the purpose of God who from eternity planned and promised the salvation Christ now offers us.

The gospel message, the Word of God, is preached, taught, read, made visible in the sacraments, explained in books, and embodied in the life of the Christian community. Experiences of Christian worship and fellowship can mediate the reality of the things of which the message speaks, or rather they may become the occasion of the Spirit's action in creating awareness of this reality. Empathy with the hearers will help the preacher, teacher, or evangelist to reach them with the message, applying it in a way that the Spirit will use to give knowledge of need and of God's grace. Parents teaching their children gospel truths should seek a like empathy. Empathy in spiritual communication is a gift of God, and should be sought from him as such; it is essentially the ability to follow Paul in becoming all things to all men so that by all means we may save some (1 Cor. 9:19–22). Fidelity to the revealed Word and its authority is an abiding need in spreading the gospel. All this is included in the means that are objective and external to the sinner, the means that God uses to accomplish his saving purposes.

The subjective means of conversion is what the sinner is called upon to do in repenting, believing, and acting upon the promised forgiveness in Christ. It is all that God accomplishes within the person to enable him or her to overcome the pressures of unbelief, to begin centering upon the invisible and eternal realities of God despite the contention of a multitude of distractions, to struggle for self-denial against inbred self-assertion. In short, it is all that moves us from being unbelievers to becoming believers.

Evangelical faith, as we have seen, is knowledge of, assent to, and trust in Christ and God's promise of grace through him. Evangelical repentance is turning from sin, now recognized as ruinous, to a new life of following Christ in righteousness, now embraced as the only hope of life. A person comes to faith and repentance by coming to understand, believe, and perceive the application to himself or herself of the gospel message. Three questions naturally arise with respect to this coming to Christ. First, are certain people more susceptible to conversion than others? Second, how much knowledge is necessary for salvation? Third, what is the appropriate motivation and preparation for conversion?

Who Is a Likely Convert?

Critics of Christian faith have often been tempted to discount its truth on the grounds that only certain "types" of people are believers. The truth of Christian faith therefore is dissolved in and seen to be only an expression of personal need: what accounts for belief, it is claimed, is internal and not external. It is psychological and not theological. It is the result of personal preference and not of public truth. What is overlooked in all of this, however, is that there are no such patterns of belief. There are no people whom we can predict will be believers. On the contrary, what is striking and what has always been striking is the social, economic, and psychological diversity within the church. The reason is that people come to saving faith, not because of a natural disposition toward the truth, but because of the initiative of God in grace that brings into his kingdom those who are not only diverse but who, if left to themselves, would never in fact enter this kingdom. We cannot predict that some people, because of personality, psychological need, or economic circumstance, will become believers. Nor are there any whose personality or life experience can successfully insulate them from the glorious intrusion of God's grace!

Consider the Acts of the Apostles. In Acts 8–16 we meet people with vastly different backgrounds who are brought to faith in Christ in different circumstances, and yet at the end all of them share a common faith.

In chapter 8, for example, there is the account of the conversion of an Ethiopian leader. He is described as a responsible man (8:27), is on a pilgrimage, reading the Jewish scriptures (8:28), and according to the conversation reported there, he is eager to learn about the new faith (8:31, 34). This man then has considerable previous knowledge about the God of the Hebrews; he has a strong desire for further understanding and a seeming willingness and readiness to make his mind up once the issues become clear.

In the next chapter there is the well-known account of the conversion of Saul of Tarsus, which we have already considered. Again, this was a man with a detailed knowledge of Judaism and the Jewish scriptures (9:1–2), an insider who was conversant with the beliefs of the early Christians. It seems he had been moved by the martyrdom of Stephen (7:60) and the Holy Spirit employed this and his knowledge of God's Word to bring him to conviction and conversion.

Chapter 10 describes a military man, probably the equivalent of a company commander in the armed services. It is evident that he was religious, for we are told that he and his whole family worshiped God. He was obviously eager to find out more and was a ready learner when the opportunity for further instruction came from the apostle Peter.

Just a little further along in the narrative we read an account of a woman who was a worshiper of God (16:14). We are told that she met with her friends for discussion and it seems that the apostle Paul on some occasions joined this group. Once she became acquainted with the details of the Christian message she became a Christian (16:15).

Later in the same chapter, however, we have a great contrast in the stressful and traumatic circumstances surrounding the conversion of the jailer at Philippi. We know little about him, but there is no particular reason to believe he knew very much about the faith. There was an earthquake during the night. He thought the prisoners were going to escape and he was on the point of suicide. In these circumstances Paul spoke to him; we are told (16:34) he made an immediate decision.

These five episodes illustrate an enormous range of experiences and backgrounds surrounding Christian conversion. The narratives suggest an equally wide range of psychological processes and different mechanisms at work. In every case the outcome is the same: belief in God and faith in Christ. If one were to focus just on the psychological aspects of the conversions, one would probably miss the most important aspect: the truth that grips the minds of the hearers, and not only the stirring of the emotions.

This point about the variety of circumstances and backgrounds surrounding conversion could equally well be made, not from the pages of Scripture, but from studies conducted by psychologists. Over the last century there have been numerous attempts to develop a profile of a typical convert, but the search for correlations between religious beliefs and measurable personality traits has been on the whole disappointing. For example, in 1962 Professor L. B. Brown studied two hundred university students and found that the correlation between their religious beliefs and a standard measure of neuroticism was only 0.03, and between their religious beliefs and extraversion only 0.07. A much older study (1951) involved nine hundred students and found no systematic relationship between personality profile and membership in a religious group. From these and similar studies it seems clear that the relation between religiosity and general personality traits is weak. The question nevertheless remains about whether there are links between religion and specialized aspects of personality. Is there any psychological description that can be given of the "typical religious person"? The general answer seems to be that while the search has been carried out energetically, it has proved unsuccessful.

There has been a little more success in identifying specialized personality traits that may be linked to certain aspects of religious personality. To take an example of this from within the literature on religious conversion, we find that psychologists have frequently pointed to the importance of suggestibility as a possible predisposing factor. This seems to be particularly the case when one is dealing with sudden conversions. Some very old studies claim to show that those who took a conservative religious position and who were also sudden converts were more suggestible than others. However, to talk loosely about suggestion really evades the problems that one faces in defining precisely what one means by it. It appears that most current books on psychology of religion agree that there is some evidence that what Professor Eysenck has called "primary suggestibility" is more in evidence in religious people than in the remainder of the population. It has also been argued that it is more in evidence among members of revivalist and evangelical bodies. Certainly, in some of the earlier revivals there are reports of many people showing signs of bodily movement, or twitching and jerking before finally collapsing.

As regards secondary suggestibility, which is the likelihood of people remembering what has been suggested to them, there is a little indirect evidence from the study of the effects of placebo treatment in hospitals. In one study it was claimed that those who said the placebo brought about relief of their pain also reported more regular attendance at church and often were described as pillars of the church. A similar study carried out ten years later reported a correlation of 0.53 between placebo, pain relief, and religiosity.

A third form of suggestibility, social suggestibility, is related to the supposed prestige of the speaker and is reported to be greater among religious people.

But if different personality characteristics influence the nature of conversion experiences, other important factors may include a person's age at the time of conversion and his or her denominational affiliation. Extensive studies on the expression of religious belief and commitment at various ages identify differences in infancy, childhood, adolescence, young adulthood, middle life, and old age. If these studies are correct, a person's age may affect his conversion experience. Denominational attachments may also result in different conversion experiences and in the way these conversions are reported and evaluated. Without doubt there are in different denominations expected ways in which religious conversion should take place and should be reported. Detailed psychological studies are not necessary to convince one of this. One only has to go and listen to testimonies given in different denominations and in different cultures.

There is almost always a temptation to attach some sort of finality to the psychological explanation that one gives of behavior such as religious conversion at a particular time. One way to avoid falling into this trap and elevating one's own explanations to a level of finality that they do not deserve is to glance briefly at the way in which attempts to understand conversion have varied over the past hundred years.

One of William James's lasting contributions in his classic book, *The Varieties of Religious Experience*, written at the end of the last century, was his classification of religious people into the "healthy minded" and the "morbid minded."

He thought these were probably related to factors of temperament and personality. James saw conversion as a perfectly normal aspect of adolescent development in which subconscious maturing processes lead to unification of the self. J. B. Pratt (in *The Religious Consciousness* [1924]) claimed to identify certain stages of religious development from the primitive to the intellectual and the emotional, which he thought were evident in all religions. By contrast, his contemporary, J. H. Leuba (in *The Psychological Study of Religion* [1912]), took a much more critical stance in his evaluation of religion. He believed it could be treated entirely from a naturalistic standpoint and contended that the religious life can be explained exclusively in terms of certain fundamental principles of general psychology. About the same time, R. H. Thouless in his *Introduction to the Psychology of Religion* followed in the same tradition as James. His particular contribution was the way in which he identified factors that he thought were involved in leading to religious belief and the different roles played by conscious and unconscious processes.

The biggest stir, of course, was made by Sigmund Freud when he turned his attention to religion and published the results in *Totem and Taboo* (1913); *Moses and Monotheism* (1939); and *The Future of an Illusion* (1934). He also had things to say about religion in *Civilization and Its Discontents* (1939). Freud had no doubt that religion was some sort of interim social neurosis that mankind would outgrow through education, through an increased ability to cope with the world, and by remaining in touch with reality. For this reason he emphasized how past religious behavior had offered a means of escape from the realities of life. Also in the psychoanalytic tradition but on a quite different track was Carl Jung. For him religion was not a matter of theological concepts but primarily of experience. After comparing and contrasting the view of Freud and Jung on religion, G. S. Spinks in 1963 wrote that for Freud "religion was an obsessional neurosis"; for Jung, "the absence of religion" was the chief contributing factor to adult psychological disorders. And neither man changed his view! This summing-up by Spinks well illustrates that one's perspective from a psychological point of view is highly likely to color the interpretation one ends with in the analysis of religious behavior, including conversion and the particular explanation given for it.

Although much less well known than the contribution of Freud and Jung, Gordon Allport's *The Individual and His Religion* (1950) made a significant contribution to the field. Unlike those of Freud and Jung, Allport's views were underpinned by considerable empirical data concerning the way in which religious beliefs emerged and how religious behavior took place. Perhaps inevitably the publicity was given to the more extreme views such as those presented by William Sargant in *Battle for the Mind* and *The Mind Possessed*, as well as the views expressed by a Harvard psychologist, B. F. Skinner.

Most noteworthy in Sargant's contributions were his attempts to link psychological studies of brainwashing with religious conversion. He believed that suggestion and brainwashing operate in large evangelistic meetings, and he attempted to identify some of the effective ingredients. Evangelists were given considerable prestige, build-up, and wide publicity beforehand. They spoke with great conviction and fervor in a meeting preceded by the repetitive singing of emotional hymns and choruses and a background of bright lights, massed choirs, and stirring music with a strong rhythmic beat. It was in these circumstances, said Sargant, that physical and psychological stresses are skillfully applied, so that they produce dramatic changes in feeling, behavior, and, ultimately, beliefs. Sargant argued that brainwashing phenomena are especially evident

78

in the meetings of the snake-handling sects in the southern states of America. When emotional exhaustion had paved the way to heightened suggestibility, beliefs were implanted and commitment was called for. There may well be some truth in some of the speculations that Sargant gave us about possible physiological processes underlying the behavior going on in these meetings, but it certainly does not tell us anything about the truth of the beliefs that were arrived at.

What is interesting about this very brief review of differing views over the past hundred years is that, in general, the explanations offered reflect psychologists' preoccupation with particular psychological theories that were currently in vogue. First was the psychoanalytical era with Freud and Jung; it was followed by the empirical era with Allport and other writers. Next were some of the psychophysiological explanations popular in the early 1950s and applied by Sargant, and then, of course, the behaviorist ones much in vogue in the 1950s and early 1960s when Skinner was at his peak. Today we are more likely to look for explanations of religious beliefs and behavior in terms of cognitive theories. That this is the case is well illustrated in L. B. Brown's book, *Advances in the Psychology of Religion* (1985).

The empirical evidence that we have, then, does not suggest there is a particular kind of person from whom we could expect a conversion experience. Furthermore, psychology itself is in sufficient flux that its models of understanding the person need to be employed with caution and reserve. What we can say is that people come into a relationship with Christ from an array of life experiences, and from within the whole diversity of personality and culture, and this fact should be neither minimized nor misinterpreted.

It should not be minimized, on the one hand, by a wooden reduction of the conversion process to a standardized form.

A crisis conversion—a conversion that is sudden, a conversion that occurs at the front of the church or an arena—is not the only way, nor even the model way, in which people are savingly drawn to Christ. There are multiple routes toward Christ, some slow and some fast, some higher in emotion, others higher in rational content, but all in the end making the same submission, receiving the same grace, and entering the same family of God.

On the other hand, this diversity should not be misinterpreted. Diversity of approach is not a diversity of gospel. Different paths toward Christ are not different religious roads to him. Christ is not hidden in secularism, or in Hinduism, or in political action, even that in the interests of the best causes. There are not multiple ways to God. Christ remains the only way, even though people and cultures differ. There is only one Lord and one faith, one God and one work of atonement, one unique Son and one conquest of evil on the cross. It is only to him that we come and in our submission he is believed in the same way through the same gospel by all.

How Much Do We Need to Know?

How much do we need to know to be converted? The answer has to be given in functional terms. We need to know enough to make us certain, through the Spirit's convincing and convicting action, that we need a new life that is right with God, and that the only way to have such a life is to trust absolutely in the mercy and direction of Jesus Christ as living and personal Savior and Lord. In our relationship with others there is constantly more cognitive awareness than people can verbalize and more situational insight than was ever imparted by the utterances of others. We need not wonder at instances of genuine faith and repentance resulting from amazingly little—we would have said, quite inadequate—formal instruction. (Some episodes in Jesus's ministry might seem to illustrate this, although the gospel narratives are also quite condensed: Luke 5:18–25; 7:37–50; 8:43–48; 17:12–19; 18:35–43; 19:1–10). Faithful preachers, teachers, and evangelists will conscientiously labor to instill full understanding of the whole gospel—creation, sin, God's holiness and love, incarnation and atonement, repentance and faith, new life in Christ, and the church. They will look to God to bless the truth that they teach, and not expect anyone to be converted without adequate knowledge. At the same time, however, they will be prepared to find that God has gone ahead of them and has blessed very little formal knowledge, producing real and virile faith in Christ.

This general affirmation needs, however, to be placed within our understanding about culture and within our knowledge of how people process information, in this case information about themselves and Christ.

Culture

Cultures are the collective ways in which people organize, interpret, and value their life together. In the affluent West, owning a Cadillac or a house in the Bahamas or wintering in warm climates carries certain connotations. Culture is a language that we all intuitively understand.

But cultures also create ways of organizing and thinking about information. For example, English-speaking people divide the rainbow into six colors: red, orange, yellow, green, blue, violet (some add indigo). People from Telugu, on the other hand, divide it into two: hot colors (red, orange, and part of yellow) and cold colors (the rest of yellow, green, blue, violet). They use adjectives to make finer distinctions. And when it comes to the broad categories for comprehending the world and its experience, there are generally recognized to be three basic mindsets: bounded, fuzzy, and relational. Bounded sets consist of things in the same category; categories are set off from one another. Westerners usually think in bounded sets. For example, one kind of fruit is an apple, another is an orange, and they are different from one another. As applied to conversion, this approach stresses the difference between being in and being out of Christ and defines carefully by doctrinal structure—things to be believed—what it means to be in Christ. Those who accept these beliefs become a bounded set (Christians) whereas those who do not remain another bounded set (non-Christians).

Fuzzy sets work by analogy and have no clear lines. A good illustration might be a rheostat. In terms of understanding belief, one might place on the one end "no belief" and on the other "full belief" and argue that almost everyone falls on a continuum between the two extremes. In cultures like that of India, fuzzy sets prevail. When conversion is construed in this way, it leads people to think that the transition from Hinduism to Christianity is gradual with slow growth into faith as a process.

Relational sets define people, not in terms of their own thinking, but in relation to another. Thus "children" refers to people who are related to "parents"; "husbands" are men related to "wives"; and a positive magnetic pole is one that is attracted to a negative pole. A particular group of people are brothers and sisters, not because of what they are intrinsically, but because they are offspring of the same parents. From this perspective, to convert is to change directions or relationships. It is to leave one relationship for another. In religious terms it is to turn from one god to another. In Christian terms it is to turn from the god of self, or any other god, and to submit to Jesus the Lord.

Bounded categories are said to be characteristic of Western thinking but, as it turns out, Western thinking is in this way also Christian. The Bible is passionately interested in truth and insists that it is God himself who will ultimately preserve the distinctions between truth and error. Christian faith is, therefore, doctrinally formed; to be a Christian is to believe certain things and not to believe others. And Christian faith is preserved only as these biblical formulations are preserved:

> So then, brethren, stand firm and hold to the traditions which you were taught by us (2 Thess. 2:15). Now we command you, brethren, in the name of the Lord Jesus Christ, that you keep away from any brother who is living in idleness and not in accord with the tradition you received from us (2 Thess. 3:6). I commend you because you . . . maintain the traditions even as I have delivered them to you (1 Cor. 11:2). Follow the pattern of the sound words which you have heard from me, in the faith and love which are in Christ Jesus (2 Tim. 1:13; cf. 2 Tim. 4:3; Titus 1:9, 13).

Indeed, in a fine study entitled *The Pattern of Christian Truth*, H. E. W. Turner has shown that in the early centuries heresy and orthodoxy were related as parasite and host. Heresy (the parasite) could exist only as it existed off orthodoxy (the host) by denying, diluting, distorting, and adding to that orthodoxy. But this was possible only if orthodoxy was a discernible, defined position—in short, a bounded set. And it was.

The cultural approach to knowledge that has the least affinity with the biblical position is the fuzzy set, characteristic of much Eastern thought but also now entering the West. The torrent of theological thought that is universalistic in outcome is invariably predicted on fuzzy-set categories where there are no sharp boundaries but only a continuum, a gradation of positions that are either more or less.

It is true, of course, that conversion does involve a movement toward God as well as a process of growing in him. In this respect, fuzzy-set thinking may seem compatible with biblical thought. However, there is a fatal flaw in fuzzy-set thinking: a clear demarcation between truth and error, between being outside of Christ and being in, is obscured. Conversion does indeed mean movement toward Christ, but until we have yielded to him and accepted by faith his gracious death in our place, we are not safe or saved. We are still outside of Christ, no matter how much we may have moved toward him.

Relational thinking, by contrast, does make connections with the biblical picture, for the gospel does call us to forsake one allegiance—our self and its extension in idolatry—and forge a new allegiance with Christ. What we have to see, however, is that the cognitive and relational components in the gospel are not alternative routes to the same end, but the parallel lines that must be traveled simultaneously and in relationship to one another if we are to know Christ. Christ is not experienced in any form of belief; he is not to be found in Hinduism, or Buddhism, or secularism. He is to be found only through the truths of the Christian gospel. It is these truths to which assent must be given in order that Christ might be trusted.

Process

How, then, do we come into saving faith? What is the process? There is, of course, no "model" experience, for culture, personality, and life experience greatly influence how a person comes to Christ. There are a number of ways to view this process.

Alan Tippett has noted a common sequence that may be brief or long in its unfolding. There are two stages in this progression. First, there is a slowly developing awareness within the person that he or she is adrift, estranged from God. At this stage a problem is being identified. Following it is a second stage, one of consideration, when the essentials of faith, cognitively or doctrinally framed, are considered as a possible solution to the problem. This, under the Spirit's guidance and because of his work, leads to the acceptance of Christ and his death and submission to him as Lord.

M. Heirich suggests a model for understanding conversion that is based on Thomas Kuhn's understanding of the development of scientific theories. Kuhn argued that scientists work with various theoretical models of knowledge which, while not perfect, are sufficiently coherent to provide a framework for research. Gradually, however, as knowledge develops, inconsistencies are detected that may initially extend the model. If they become too substantial, the existing paradigm is challenged as inadequate and a whole new paradigm emerges. The emergence of the theory of relativity is a good example of a profound change in model that became necessary as the evidence for traditional physics was no longer adequate. The newly-emerging model allows for new predictions and eventually a radical position in science becomes the accepted wisdom.

Heirich sees a close parallel in the realignment of thinking that goes on in the consideration prior to conversion, leading to the ultimate abandonment of the old worldview in favor of a more satisfying one. Indeed, to adopt the language of experience, Kuhn calls this a "paradigm shift," a "conversion experience that cannot be forced." Rather than reacting with hostility against new thinking, it becomes necessary to embrace the new paradigm as one with future promise.

An attempt to test this hypothesis was made in 1986 by an Australian, G. P. Cobiac. He investigated responses of recent converts to a Catholic charismatic group, comparing them with two control groups. The results of Cobiac's investigation generally supported Heirich's hypothesis. Converts tended to view their past more negatively and to be weaker and more passive than members of the control groups. They became more ready to attribute positive outcomes in their lives to the intervention of God, while a non-Christian control group more readily made negative attributions to God. A significant difference was also found in the language structure of converts, who used metaphor and content having specific meaning within a Christian belief system—or, we might say, they learned to speak "the language of Zion." Christian faith, in other words, was beginning to "make sense" of their experience, past and present, and it had become the route for looking with hope into the future.

How much knowledge is necessary for conversion? The answer is different for every person and must be formed functionally. We need as much knowledge as will bring us to an awareness of ourselves as sinners, sufficient knowledge to understand how Christ will "solve" the problem we are sensing, enough knowledge to see how the world will look from within Christ, and enough knowledge to know what is asked of us as we believe the gospel and what will be required of us after we believe it. Providing this knowledge not only establishes the basis for a relationship with Christ but it also prevents evangelism from trading on misapprehension or employing manipulative devices. The convert comes into faith responsibly and the evangelist can be confident that the gospel has not been offered under false pretenses.

Should We Prepare for Conversion?

In what ways can a person prepare for conversion, how much preparation is necessary, and what are the proper motivations in coming to Christ? These constitute the third set of questions which we need to ask. Once more, the only possible answer is the functional one: the preparation that is needed, along with belief that the gospel is true, is a sufficient falling out of love with sin and sufficient gratitude to Jesus for opening the door to a new and godly way of living. This is not, however, an endorsement of the doctrine (feared by many, though held by very few) that only one who has undergone a long period of heavy contrition is qualified to come to Christ, or will be received by him. The legalistic "preparationism" that was allegedly taught by the Puritans and others who supposedly stressed the need for deep conviction of sin and labored to induce it is, in truth, a figment of the critics' imagination. The Puritans (and their admirers, past and present) actually maintained that only one who has come thoroughly to hate sin can turn wholeheartedly from it to Christ. Contrition is necessitated not by the terms of the gospel, which calls us to Christ directly, but by the state of the fallen human heart. God uses the law to pave the way for the gospel by making us see not only our guilt but also the ugliness, nastiness, and repulsiveness of our previous ways, so that we cease to love them; and that sets us free to love Christ when he calls us to follow him into different ways.

The alternative is the false conversion that is illustrated by seed falling on stony ground in Jesus's parable of the soils. Today we see people who have been pressured to make decisions, who received the word of pardon and peace with joy, and who promise to follow Christ henceforth, but then find the old way of Christlessness and sin more attractive than the new way of resisting sin out of loyalty to Christ and suffering in consequence (see Heb. 12:3–4). So, they go rapidly back to their old ways. That shows that such inner conviction and change as was experienced never went deep enough to

87

make the life of sin intolerable forever after, or to produce clear understanding that Christ will only save us from sin, never in sin. If we are to avoid producing false conversions, we must make much of the law, sin, and repentance in our communication, and not press people for gestures of decision until we have done all we can to make sin hateful in their eyes and have reason to judge that they have received this part of the message. But this deep conviction of sin, like the conviction that the gospel announces realities that impinge on life, comes only from the Holy Spirit's application of the word we communicate.

Is this talk about sin and about the need to recognize our own sinfulness a pathological way of dealing with internal crises? This argument has often been made, especially by those in Freudian circles. But as is so often the case, the perspective of the psychologist seems to influence heavily what he or she will find. Psychologists who are committed to Christian faith have found evidence for thinking that conversion is not regressive and pathological but part of a normal, healthy development. Indeed, in one study mentally ill people were discovered to be significantly less religious than the general population. The truth is, of course, that religious faith can become a part of, or be the evidence of, a person's disorientation, even as it can be the cause and consequence of a person's reorientation. Defining what is and is not religious is so problematic and it is complicated by the intrusion of the psychologist's own views. The case for seeing conversion as retrogressive has not been successfully made. There is, however, solid evidence for seeing that religion, specifically Christian faith, is able to bring a person through crisis to a wholeness and a constructive approach to life.

There is, however, a convergence between the functioning of the law and the shape of the inner life, if we understand the latter in terms of needs. In his study of 3,574 converts, R. Wallace discovered that faith answers four basic needs: social, stability, solidarity, and influence. A person with social needs feels that others do not sufficiently appreciate him or her. A person who is going through life transitions and is feeling battered by uncertainty needs stability. A person who has not inherited solid or foundational values from the family needs solidarity. A person with influence needs lacks emotional links to those who have strong faith.

Some people do not sense these needs very strongly, for they perceive themselves to be free of deficits. Others may have been so traumatized by their upbringing that, though they sense these needs deeply, conversion is almost unthinkable. Conversion calls for trust, but their whole inner life is built around distrust.

These needs correlate with the framework provided by the law. The key to social alienation (we are not appreciated sufficiently by others) and personal alienation (we sense ourselves to be adrift, to have no moorings, to have no clear focus, no solid core to our lives) is alienation from God. Once we understand that we are alienated from God—that we have substituted ourselves for him, have created our own norms and values in place of his, have seen ourselves as the center of life instead of him—then we easily understand that these inner needs are consequences of our sinful behavior. These consequences, these deficits, are addressed in the gospel that serves, not simply as an addition to our lives, but as the reordering agent that establishes the life on such a footing that the deficits can be addressed by God himself.

What we have seen, then, is that a decision for Christ is not the real measure of a conversion, although a conversion may occur in and through such a decision. Decisions undertaken with insufficient self-awareness, awareness of ourselves as sinners before God (however that awareness translates into felt needs), are decisions whose reality will be hollow. Decisions undertaken in the absence of a sufficient knowledge of God, his truth, and his Christ are decisions that will likely be malformed and so will probably lack direction and hence staying power. Decisions that occur in either of these ways are decisions brought about by pressures that should be considered manipulative: the crowd or circle of friends who exert psychological pressure or the evangelist who does a "hard sell" and is so charismatic in personality or in presentation that the convert is drawn to the point of decision irresistibly. This person, let it be noted, is also being drawn foolishly and, perhaps, unethically. Decisions are not what counts. What counts is that there are men and women who, knowing themselves to be rebels and alienated from God, have sought in his Christ forgiveness and acceptance and, having sought and trusted, have been renewed by the Spirit and are impelled on to a life of truthfulness and love.

4

The Church's View of Conversion

That conversion means change, a turning from sin and a turning toward God, has been recognized through much of the church's life. How and why this occurs has, however, been debated. Does it occur because of baptism, confession, and priestly absolution or, in the modern period, when one is pressed for a decision? And how is Christ's work on the cross and the Spirit's work of renewal related to this? Does Christ simply make his grace available through the church's channels of sacrament or priestly function, or is it accessible only through the exercise of faith? And is the Spirit's work of renewal before or after the exercise of faith? The interpenetration of these questions and the different answers to them have shifted the patterns of understanding conversion around so that there really is no discernible, uniform pattern.

What needs to be traced in this chapter, then, is not so much the deviations from the biblical model but the variations within the evangelical understanding of that model. And we need to begin with Augustine because it was from him that both Luther and Luther's opponents found their inspiration.

These two models of understanding—conversion by grace through faith and conversion dispensed through the church—were combined in Augustine's thought, but the passage of time thoroughly disengaged them. Having noted that, we shall follow the line of evangelical thinking that was first formed in Augustine as he reflected upon the New Testament, was given powerful expression in the Reformation, was refined during the period of classical orthodoxy, and has been increasingly reduced in the modern period.

Augustine

Augustine was not the first person in the post-apostolic period to think about conversion; he was not the first person to be converted. But he did bring to his own experience extraordinary powers of analysis, a depth of understanding, and a range of theological knowledge that make him a good point of departure for our consideration.

We can, in fact, find evidence of three "conversions" in Augustine's life. These were intellectual, moral, and ecclesiastical in nature, but their occurrence was also part of the unfolding of Augustine's life. Augustine was not really raised as a pagan. His father was a pagan, but his mother was a Christian and the dominant religious influence on him. In his adolescence he drifted away from Christianity, both intellectually and morally. Intellectually he rejected the simplicity of Catholic Christianity and was drawn to the sophistication of Cicero and the elitism of Manicheism. Morally, he became dissolute, taking a concubine. In his *Confessions*, he records the process by which God brought him back. He tells of his intellectual pilgrimage from disillusionment with Manichean dualism to a period of skepticism. He emerged from his skepticism through a discovery of Platonism and through a renewed interest in Christianity because of the preaching of Ambrose, the bishop of Milan. Augustine confessed that through Platonism and Ambrose he came to understand and accept the truth. His *intellectual conversion* had occurred.

But a moral problem—primary for Augustine—remained. "It is one thing to see the land of peace . . . and quite another to hold to the way that leads there" (7.21). "My desire now was not to be more sure of You but more steadfast in You" (8.1). He accepted the truth but he felt chained by a perverse will to carnal habit: "For the law of sin is the fierce force of habit, by which the mind is drawn and held even against its will, and yet deservedly because it had fallen willfully into the habit" (8.5).

Augustine experienced a growing sense of frustration with his inability to overcome his sexual lusts. One day he was reading and meditating alone in a walled garden. He heard a child's voice saying, "Take and read; take and read." He picked up the Scriptures and read Romans 13:13, "Not in rioting and drunkenness, not in chambering and impurities, not in contention and envy, but put ye on the Lord Jesus Christ and make not provision for the flesh in its concupiscences" (8.12). This dramatic experience marked his *moral conversion* and was an occasion of great joy: "By your gift I had come totally not to will what I had willed but to will what You willed" (9.1).

This moral conversion led Augustine to embrace ascetic Christianity and moral rigorism. Just before his conversion, Augustine had been reading the life of Saint Anthony, the Egyptian hermit. In describing his own change, Augustine wrote, "For You converted me to Yourself so that I no longer sought a wife nor any of this world's promises" (8.12). For

Augustine and for many others, genuine moral conversions came to be marked most fully by embracing an ascetic life. By the fourth century, especially after the conversion of Constantine, ascetic Christianity was becoming the response of serious Christians to the formalism and nominalism of the church.

Still, Augustine believed his conversion was not complete: "Thus in that depth I recognized the act of Your will, and I gave praise to Your name, rejoicing in faith. But this faith would not let me feel safe about my past sins, since Your baptism had not yet come to remit them" (9.4). The evening before Easter, April 24, 387, Ambrose baptized Augustine and many others. Augustine reflected: "We were baptized, and all anxiety as to our past life fled away" (9.6). This was his *ecclesiastical conversion*.

The *Confessions* also show Augustine's understanding that his conversion was entirely the work of God's grace. He wrote the work as his testimony to God's electing and pursuing grace. His conviction about the sovereignty of God in salvation and his rejection of any role for human free will was strengthened in the Pelagian controversy. Augustine's victory over Pelagius established the label *Augustinian* as synonymous with virtue and *Pelagian* with evil. Yet Augustine's mature position on predestination and grace was not always maintained in the church.

In strikingly apt phrase, B. B. Warfield observed that the Protestant Reformation represented the revolt of Augustine's doctrine of grace against his doctrine of the church. It was a revolt, especially on the Reformed side, against seeing grace channeled through the sacraments and it was a revolt, in all Reformational expressions, against the notion that predestination trickled only through the narrow crevices of church ordinances. It was, by contrast, an affirmation of Augustine's grasp upon human lostness, bondage to what is dark and wrong, the indispensability of grace, the glory of the gospel because of him in whom the Good News took and takes form. Thus it is that we need to see how these paths diverged: on the one side, conversion increasingly was understood as occurring in the church, through the church, because of the church; on the other side, conversion was seen as occurring by grace, through faith, because of God's sovereign and direct initiative.

Conversion through the Church

The development we need to note first was one in which the church increasingly managed and controlled the dispensation of grace. This took place initially as saving grace was seen to be conveyed sacramentally; to be converted became synonymous with entry into the church at baptism. Then attention shifted to the removal of postbaptismal sin through penance. After baptism, the convert had to settle accounts with God for sins committed. This occurred through forms of discipline, humiliation, privation, and even flagellation (in serious cases) as the "flesh" was subdued (so it was thought). In two of his treatises, Tertullian set out the theory for a practice widespread in the third century. Tertullian's explanation had two prongs to it. First, sins create debits and so the offsetting credit of good works had to be provided in this life or in purgatory. Second, in penance, an eternal punishment for sins is discharged in the present in a temporal form and thus the account can be squared. This theory provided the framework for Anselm's *Cur Deus Homo*, in which he argued that Christ accrued a massive amount of merit on the cross, none of which he needed for himself, and so this could be dispersed to sinners who—and here Anselm's theory was a great improvement over Tertullian's theology—are not able to accrue merit for themselves because sin is not a temporal liability but a dishonoring of the eternal God. Later, penance became a marketable commodity in the form of indulgences. It was just this abuse that so angered Luther. An indulgence peddler, a "braggart" (as Luther calls him), made the rounds selling an indulgence with an oft-repeated promise: "The moment the coin in the coffer rings, A soul from purgatory springs."

Conversion, in other words, no longer involved the agony of soul, the searching for God, the grace, the repentance, the submission to God in Christ, that courses through Augustine's *Confessions*. The word *conversion* was now used in many other church-oriented ways. In the sixth and seventh centuries, it referred to joining a monastery; in the twelfth century, Peter Lombard used it to describe the supernatural change in the eucharistic elements. Thomas Aquinas used it of "every movement of the will of God." He went on to speak of three conversions: the drawing of sinners by grace to God, the entry of that sinner into grace, and the habit of living in grace. Each stage, of course, was accomplished through and by the church.

For Aquinas, the intellectual element in conversion was acceptance of church teaching. Faith is assent to the truth. It is an essential element in salvation, but is not enough by itself. Faith is a habit of grace in the soul, but by itself it is unformed faith. As the body without a soul is only a corpse, so faith without its form is dead. The form of faith is love. Love enlivens faith and makes it saving faith. Love makes the habit of grace meritorious and acceptable to God. Faith and love together are an infusion of grace that result in justification and conversion. This theology shows the virtual identification of justification and sanctification that characterizes Roman Catholicism. Conversion is moral improvement, as well as forgiveness, and it is this that makes one acceptable to God. The infusion of grace occurs preeminently through the sacraments. The foundational sacrament is baptism, in which spiritual "generation" occurred; therefore, Aquinas said, it "opens the gate of heaven." And postbaptismal sins were accounted for by penance.

In medieval theology, the stress upon the sacraments was intended as a stress upon the objectivity of saving grace. Since at least the sixth century onward, Augustine's profound understanding of the nature and consequences of sin substantially disappeared. In its place was a shallow moralism that defined sins as simply infractions of the rules. Sin could be eliminated by the compensating weight of good works. And underlying this moralism was a semi-Pelagianism that compromised the biblical understanding of how sin cripples our capacity to seek, love, or serve God outside of his sovereign redeeming work in our lives. The combination of this semi-Pelagianism and this shallow moralism, coupled with the confusion over how God's grace is received, resulted in justification being misconstrued as a righteousness produced during life rather than a righteousness conferred by Christ. Another way of saying this is that medieval theology had no doctrine of justification in a biblical sense but replaced it by a doctrine of sanctification. In so doing, it called upon baptized Christians to energize the grace conferred on them in baptism by cooperation and works of love. This view, in which God and the sinner are both needed to pull on the rope, was later to be expounded by Bellarmine as "congruism." Today we call it synergism. It was against this view that Luther fired off his blasts in the interest of preserving the monogism of grace.

The Reformation Tradition

Even before his famous protest, the invitation to debate the ninety-five theses, Luther wrote a withering attack on current ideas of salvation in a treatise entitled *Disputation Against Scholastic Theology*. He dismissed categorically the notion that salvation is a process of slowly ascending to God in a cooperative action between God and the sinner. Luther argued that nothing precedes God's grace except ill will on the sinner's part. This ill-will so captures and permeates the whole person that the sinner can take no step toward God until God himself has liberated the sinner. Later, Luther defended this position against Erasmus in *On the Freedom of the Will*. Erasmus seemed throughout to think he and Luther were talking about psychology and determinism: whether God accomplishes his will through sinners as a puppeteer works through his puppets. Luther was discussing soteriology, not psychology, and asking whether we contribute to our salvation in a cooperative action with God. The answer he gave, not surprisingly, was that we do not because we cannot.

Luther arrived at his view of salvation by a route not unlike that of Augustine. As a young monk, Luther felt crushed by the thought of God's righteousness and the demands God made on him. Indeed, he tells us that when he heard the word *Christ* (his judge), he trembled and turned pale. But his study of Scripture led him to realize that when Paul wrote of the "righteousness of God" (Rom. 1:17), he referred not to the righteousness that God demands, but to the righteousness that God *gives* in Christ. This breakthrough resulted in his conversion: "Here I felt that I was altogether born again and had entered paradise itself through open gates." He went on to say that anyone wanting to be converted had to "become terrified and die," had to have "an abandoned and trembling conscience." Only then would this person be ready to take hold of God's consolation—not anything any sinner has accomplished but what God has done in his Son whose "consoling compassion" can be appropriated through faith by "terrified sinners." Here Augustine's understanding of sin, and behind Augustine what Paul and the New Testament had declared, was recovered and applied! Here was the agony of a sinner who learns that he is utterly bereft of help from within and, in seeing that, casts himself totally upon the substitutionary work of Christ for justification.

It remains to be said, however, that conversion itself was not a dominant concept for Luther; for him, the focus was more objective than subjective, more on what Christ has done in justifying us than on how we experience this in regeneration, more on the faith by which we should take hold of Christ than on how we should decide for him, more upon God than upon ourselves. Still, he did speak of conversion. He used the word *conversion* in three ways: first, of baptism; second, of repentance and contrition that is to be repeated (some Lutherans still speak of "daily conversion"); third, of the moment of dramatic personal transformation as in his own tower experience when he felt the gates of paradise had been opened to him through Christ.

On the Reformed side, we find substantial identification with Luther's point of view but also some divergence from it. Calvin, too, was a Christ-centered thinker and in this respect he made two important points. First, the continual conversion (turning from sin and self to God and righteousness) in which the Christian's lifelong repentance consists is entirely God's work, inasmuch as it is the expression of a sinful heart that God has now made new and keeps new. Our "good works," to the extent that they are good, are thus God's gifts, not our achievements. Second, the active turning to himself that God works in Christians is the fruit of faith—a God-wrought disposition of assured and heartfelt trust in God as Father, in Christ as mediator, and in God's promise of mercy as truth applying to oneself. In substance these emphases correspond exactly to those of Luther, in *On the Freedom of the Will*, where he controverts the idea of meritorious good works.

Calvin's own conversion has been the subject of speculation precisely because he says so little about it. He simply tells us that at a certain time God subdued his hard heart and made him teachable. But conversion was, nevertheless, very important in his theology. He used the word *conversion* as a synonym for repentance and sanctification. In the *Institutes*, Calvin discussed the doctrine of faith: "With good reason, the sum of the gospel is held to consist in repentance and forgiveness of sins . . . now, both repentance and forgiveness of sins—that is, newness of life and free reconciliation—are conferred on us by Christ, and both are attained by us through justification and sanctification." For him repentance and conversion are really the same as sanctification, and thus the result of faith: "Now it ought to be a fact beyond controversy that repentance not only constantly follows faith, but is also born of faith" (3.3.1). In these terms Calvin clearly identified conversion with moral change, but sharply distinguished it from justification. Baptism was but the sign and seal of initiation into the church but did not affect that initiation.

Calvin's approach to understanding conversion was followed in the Heidelberg Catechism (1563). The catechism is divided into three sections: (1) sin and misery, (2) deliverance from sin, and (3) gratitude for deliverance. Near the beginning of the third section, question 88 asks, "What is involved in genuine repentance or conversion?" The answer is, "Two things: the dying away of the old self, and the coming-to-life of the new." Here, following Calvin, conversion is identified with repentance and refers to the *entire process of sanctification* in the Christian life. That process must of course have a beginning, but the use of conversion in this context does not stress the beginning over the lifelong dimension of conversion.

Calvin and theologians in the early Reformed tradition expressed themselves somewhat differently from the Lutheran tradition on the formal definition of the gospel. For Lutherans, the gospel is purely promise and calls for the response of faith. It must be preached with the law that calls for repentance. For Calvinists, the gospel is the promise of forgiveness and renewal and calls for faith and repentance. But both Lutherans and Calvinists share the same basic understanding of justification, of acceptance having been offered through Christ in whom sin was judged and from whom righteousness is received by faith. There was great stress in Luther and Calvin on faith resting on the promises of Christ. The promise brought joy and certainty into the Christian's life. Free justification through the perfect righteousness of Christ stood at the center of the Reformation.

The formal commitment to justification remained clear in the developing Reformed tradition, but some theologians developed new emphases that seemed to move justification out of the center of Christian theology and experience. Some of the Puritan theologians, for example, taught in ways that changed Calvin's approach. The most obvious instance is in the doctrine of assurance. Calvin clearly, even passionately, taught that assurance was the essence of faith. Faith is assured as it rests in the promises of God. Some Puritans taught that assurance was not of the essence of faith, but a goal of faith. They also shifted attention from the promises of God in the Scriptures as the foundation of assurance, to the believer's *experience* of sanctifying grace (the practical syllogism). They argued that their approach to assurance would enhance assurance for believers. But the effect seems to have been the opposite. Assurance became more and more of a struggle. Experience became more and more important.

The stress on experience and the growing concern about formalism in the Christian church led to a heightened focus among many Puritans on conversion, still understood as the moral renewal of the Christian. The concern can be seen in works like Joseph Alleine's *Alarm to Unconverted Sinners* (1671) and Richard Baxter's *Treatise on Conversion* (1657). For both, conversion remained basically a moral matter, entered into instantaneously, but in both of these Puritans there was the sense of the *difficulty* of conversion. What they meant, apparently, was that grace was not to be taken for granted; God should not be presumed upon; in the end, the broad road to destruction would prove appealing to more people than the narrow road to life.

This concern led many of the Puritans to stress the need for preparation. By this they affirmed that while salvation is sovereignly initiated, it is not given until sufficient reflection upon sin has occurred, until the sinner has lost all hope in himself or herself and knows that God alone is the way to life. Sometimes this interest did result in a technique whose outcome was the passivity of the sinner who lost sight of the urgency to take hold of the promised forgiveness. Yet, the Puritan concern that sin be understood and that it be forsaken as a precondition for the exercise of faith seems quite preferable to the common evangelical view today of conversion as a divinely triggered psychological event whereby a lost sinner passes from death to life. This view, while contradicting nothing that Luther or Calvin taught, is more human-centered, experience-oriented, and evangelistically angled than the Reformers' teaching on repentance and faith ever was, or the Puritan concern that the heart of the gospel is not to be bartered away through an insufficient understanding of what it is we are saved from and what salvation cost God.

Revivals and Missions

In the eighteenth century, the currents of Reformation theology, Puritan spirituality, and Pietist intensity flowed into the revivals that are now known as the Great Awakening that ignited the eastern seaboard of the United States and many parts of Great Britain. Once again, evangelical faith was especially crystallized through the struggle and subsequent ministries of people who had sought for God in other ways. Both George Whitefield and John Wesley were churchmen, people acquainted with the church and its sacraments. Both, however, needed to be converted and were: Whitefield in 1735 and Wesley in 1738 after having read the preface to Luther's commentary on Romans in which justification was expounded. Both men began to preach their new sense of faith and conversion. Many churchmen considered their message shocking and closed their pulpits to them. Whitefield led the way in England in open-air preaching and Wesley followed.

In some ways their theologies diverged. Wesley became an Arminian and taught Christian perfection. As a matter of fact, he had believed in the possibility of "sinless perfection" before his conversion and that experience seemed only to heighten Wesley's conviction on this matter. Whitefield did not, and his theology instead reiterated the interests of the Reformation, with the concern to protect God's sovereign grace in the salvation of sinners.

They were united, however, on two points that set them off from most of their Puritan forebears. First, they both called for conversion without delay. They did not teach, as many Puritans had, that ordinarily there should be a period of despairing over sins before conversion. Second, they seemed to teach that assurance was inherent in faith, not a goal to be pursued after conversion.

The preaching of Whitefield, Wesley, and others was remarkable for the revitalization that it brought to churches in England and America. Their preaching broke through the indifference and cold formalism of many in their day. They reached out to elements of society that were largely unreached by the churches. And they brought into focus, in a way that had not happened in the Reformation period, the centrality and importance of the new birth. The doctrine of justification was affirmed and affirmed without reservation, but the emphasis lay more upon regeneration.

Already in this development lay the seeds of the modern reduction of the gospel. There are two dangers here that can seduce even earnestly pious people. If the Reformation focus on conversion is retained, in which the term is used broadly of the whole moral and spiritual transformation, then faith easily becomes moralistic. Faith can lose its dynamic and experiential quality and become simply the things that ought to be done. On the other hand, when conversion comes to refer primarily or exclusively to the initial Christian experience of faith, the danger is that the moral element of Christianity (as well as the doctrinal) will be reduced to a minimal level. Further, the sacramental ministry of the church will be seen as irrelevant to conversion. The proper balance—as Wesley and Whitefield seemed to sense in their better moments—was manifested in the Reformation with its preaching of faith and repentance, but that is not a balance that we always see in today's evangelical practice.

The transition toward this narrower view of what is entailed in coming to know Christ and his saving work did not occur immediately, nor is it without exceptions in today's evangelical world. Much of the older, fuller theology was preserved. This was true, for example, of the extraordinary missionary activity in the nineteenth century to which Kenneth Latourette devoted three of the seven volumes in *A History of the Expansion of Christianity.*

Protestant missionaries have always regarded the conversion of the heathen as the primary goal of their labors. They considered it to be the distinct mark of the evangelical—in contrast to the Roman Catholic—concept and practice of missions. On account of their sacramental understanding of grace, Catholic missionaries often hastened to baptize people in great masses, leaving their deeper introduction into the faith to the later stage of their pastoral education as church members. The secretary of the American Board of Commissioners for Foreign Missions, Rufus Anderson, one of the earliest Protestant missiologists, pointed out that Francis Xavier, the Jesuit missionary, had applied superficial methods and, therefore, did not reap any permanent fruit from his extensive labors. Protestant missionaries, Anderson argued, should avoid these mistakes by laying solid foundations. Their strategy should be to insist upon the true conversion of their heathen listeners, and then gather them into independent churches which, on account of the high spiritual quality of their members, should and in fact would be self-propagating, self-governing, and self-supporting right from the start. The famous "three-selves formula" soon became the adopted slogan of the Protestant mission strategy aiming at the establishment of indigenous churches.

According to the originators of this missionary methodology, Anderson and Henry Venn, the success or failure of a mission would wholly depend on the observation of their cardinal condition: the true conversion of the ecclesial nucleus. This idea was later developed in detail and radically propagated in the writings of the Anglican missiologist Roland Allen. He added his distinct concept of the empowering effect of the Holy Spirit, dwelling in converts no matter what their culture or their amount of formal education.

Conversion, thus, was both the theological and strategical key concept of Anglo-Saxon missiology in the nineteenth and early twentieth centuries. It was taken from the evangelical heritage of the classical revival movements and applied more or less unmodified to the conditions of the overseas mission fields. The evangelical home boards believed that the spiritual laws in God's redemptive work, which had been so marvelously effective in the recent experiences at home, were revealed in the Bible and were, therefore, timeless and universally applicable.

If there was a shift, and it appears that there was, it occurred as a result of the Second Great Awakening in America. The revival apparently began in the villages of the Connecticut River Valley in 1792, reached its peak in the 1830s and 1840s, and rumbled on intermittently until it culminated in Billy Sunday's campaigns in the early part of the twentieth century. The shift in understanding about conversion had several stages. First, evangelism moved outside the churches, not (as in the case of Wesley and Whitefield) because the churches were inhospitable, but because it really was a new kind of evangelism. Second, emphasis shifted from the older Reformational interests in the inability of the sinner and the sovereignty of grace to newer concerns (that were at least Arminian and often Pelagian) about the sinner's ability to appropriate Christ unaided. Third, there occurred a shift from evangelism that was more personal to that which was aimed at the masses, a transition made easy by the new theology (and later by television) and made necessary, it seemed, by the growth in population.

The two people with whom these changes are most readily associated are, of course, Charles Finney and D. L. Moody. Especially in the case of Moody, we see evangelism becoming international, not in the sense that it was done everywhere, but rather of one person evangelizing in many places geographically far apart.

Moody's campaigns, for which a huge movable assembly hall (Tabernacle) was constructed, were performed in three stages: the preparation, the delivery of the message, and the call for decision. During the preparation, where only his fellow workers (especially the famous gospel singer Ira Sankey) appeared on the stage, the people were warmed up emotionally by popular songs with a plain gospel message until their expectation of the main preacher had reached its summit. The delivery by Moody himself was marked by a dramatic presentation of the basic choice between the judgment of God, which was relentlessly awaiting the unrepentant sinner, and the pardoning pronouncement of grace to the believer. Although Moody would unfold the perils of being condemned to hell in most drastic terms, people reacted with neither despair nor cynicism, because they felt the preacher's passionate love for them and his genuine personal concern for their salvation that even drove him to tears.

Moody, like Finney, would then call his listeners to a straightforward decision in front of the audience. During this appeal a great number of listeners would usually respond. These results, too, were still marked by stability; the rate of backsliders was relatively low compared with the figures of his twentieth-century successors.

Yet even at this point, some of the inherent weaknesses of this approach were becoming plain. Where conversion is reduced to an experience and, indeed, an experience that can almost be induced, it is disengaged from the whole corpus of belief in which it should have found a place. Truth is replaced by experience; what Christ did on the cross (objective) becomes what Christ does in sinners (subjective); justification retreats and regeneration alone becomes the gospel. The objective means of conversion largely vanishes and the evangelist employs the subjective. The result is that each evangelist aims to reap decisions, rather than to bring humbled, penitent sinners to the only source from whom forgiveness can be had. This is all a natural outgrowth of the approach pioneered by Finney and Moody, neither of whom doubted that immediate, wholehearted repentance was possible for anyone who had been sufficiently "broken down" (Finney's phrase) by the pressure or allure of the evangelist's persuasive speech. One notes here the revival of the seventeenth-century Arminian view that moral suasion is all that is needed to induce conversion, a thesis that Augustinians and those in the Reformation and Puritan traditions denied, appealing to such passages as Romans 8:7–11; 9:14–24; Ephesians 2:1–10; and John 6:43–45. In line with this conviction, evangelists frequently orchestrate intense pressure points at the close of each meeting of each crusade, seeking to "draw in the net" and "reap the harvest." If, however, "decision" and "commitment" mean repentance and faith, and if faith and repentance can occur only as the convicting Spirit of God actually changes the person inwardly, and if the working of the Spirit is not ours to command, there is some unreality and some misdirection, as well as some manipulation, in making it appear as if coming forward for counseling, or responding with whatever other gesture is asked for, will eternally clinch, here and now, the issue of a person's conversion. Even if it is said from the platform that this is not necessarily so, the procedure itself seems to tell a different story.

Public confession of faith has helped some people to make their breach with the past decisive. It has served as the moment when all of God's convicting work came to a head and Christ was grasped through faith as the only answer to the painful dilemmas that had been felt within. The important point in this, however, is to ask what kind of gospel it is that is being believed. It is possible—indeed, it is common today—for the process of decision making, be it public or private, to be built on a gospel whose substance and whose demands are so minimal as to be unrecognizable by biblical standards.

We need to note, then, that the narrowed preaching on conversion with which we are so familiar today is not how the church has always done its gospel business. We may think that using the word *conversion* of the whole of Christian life will belittle the importance of the first act of believing; we may worry that a person could agonize before the law so long that belief in Christ is never arrived at; we may be so in awe of the exponential growth in world population that we may feel driven to introduce our own "new measures" that will make believing so easy that the proclamation of the gospel to the whole world in our generation becomes feasible. If, because of these concerns, we end up with a gospel that demands little from the believer, offers little because little needs to be received, issues in a faith that is just a notched-up sense of self-awareness, and makes few or perhaps no connections with the great issues and challenges of our day, we can say surely that ours is no longer the biblical gospel.

5

Religious Outsiders

Jews and Muslims

The Arab/Israeli wars, with their never-ending cycles of animosity, violence, revenge, and retribution, might lead one to think that Judaism and Islam have nothing in common. But this is not the case. Although these nations are politically opposed to one another, their religious beliefs (at least with respect to their origins) are not nearly so polarized.

Muhammad recognized a certain affinity between Islam and the monotheism of Judaism. The basic credal statements of Judaism—"The LORD our God is one LORD" (Deut. 6:4)— and Islam—"He is God, one, God the alone" (Sura 112:1)— are certainly similar. Just as the Jews of Jesus's day rejected the notion that there was more than one person in the Godhead, so Islam rejects the Christian doctrine of the Trinity as tritheism. Islam emphasizes reverence for an entirely transcendent God. Both Islam and Judaism revere angels as agents who mediated the revelation of God's Word. Angels revealed the Torah to Moses (Gal. 3:19; Heb. 2:2), and Muhammad is said to have received the Quran under the supervision of Gabriel (Sura 2:97/91). The Quran recognizes a number of prominent Old Testament figures as prophets: Abraham, Lot, Noah, Aaron, David, and Solomon. Although the Bible does not categorize these men as prophets, the Jewish Aggada (folklore) later gave them this status. Both religions predict a future judgment day. Each has a distinctive view of community life.

The concepts of the *umma* in Islam and of the theocratic community in early Judaism are very similar. Both have a holistic view of human existence that regulates every aspect of life for those within the community. There is no separation of the sacred and the profane, of religion and politics, or of private and public morals. The total conduct of life is determined by the dictates of God's will as revealed in Scripture and the law that is developed from it. Additionally, close similarities exist between Muslim laws and orthodox Jewish laws. For instance, both have regulations about ceremonial purity, and both have dietary laws to determine what is "clean" and "unclean" and ritual ablutions to remedy the latter. Both have obligatory duties and prescribed methods of worship (prayers, fasting, and pilgrimage). Both have social laws to regulate the life of the community, with striking similarities in the provision for the disadvantaged (orphans and widows), marriage, and the laws of inheritance. The Jewish messianic hope has its counterpart in the Islamic Mahdi, who will bring a reign of perfect justice and righteousness on earth. The Mahdi has special prominence among the Shi'ites. Finally, there are parallels in the concept and practice of the priesthood.

Although Judaism has a designated priesthood with clearly defined duties, Islam acknowledges no priestly office or appointed mediator between humans and God. In practice, however, various categories of Muslim leadership (imam, qadhi, khatib, etc.) assume certain priestly functions. These leaders receive converts into Islam and excommunicate apostates. They preside at public services; they initiate the sacrifice and rituals at the two great religious festivals; and they participate in circumcision, marriage, and funeral ceremonies. Equally important are the intercessory powers claimed for certain persons, most notably Muhammad himself, as well as Husayn and the Hidden Imam in Shi'ite Islam and the sheikhs, walis, and pirs of popular Islam.

In view of these parallels between Judaism and Islam, does the conversion of a Muslim to Christianity result in a true Muslim (*muslim* means "submitter" to God) in the same way that the conversion of a Jew is the fulfillment of that person's Jewish roots? Does the gospel complete what is lacking in Islam? Does it provide the power to accomplish the ideals of Islam (which are so similar to the ideals of Judaism) that otherwise are humanly unattainable? Converted Muslims frequently believe that they continue to worship the same God as before but with a fuller understanding of his nature.

In our terminology, should the conversion of Jews and Muslims be considered as "insider" or as "outsider" conversion? Do either Jews or Muslims possess a sufficient framework of knowledge so that the gospel becomes the last piece to fall into place in the puzzle? Or are the entire bases of the Jewish and Muslim belief systems so permeated with error that converted Jews and Muslims need to make a fresh start?

It is wisest not to answer these questions in the abstract, since a great deal depends upon the individual faith of the Muslim or Jew. Islam is not the monolithic, unified religion it is commonly supposed to be. There are at least two major streams, Sunni and Shi'ite. Each of these streams has a number of tributaries, such as Orthodox Muslims, the Folk or Popular Muslims, and Sufis. Furthermore, Islam is pervasively syncretistic in nature. From the time of Muhammad onward, a number of animistic features were incorporated into Islam, beginning with certain aspects of pre-Islamic Arab tribal religion. Now there are a great number of local variations in Islam around the world. For example, the majority of Indonesian Muslims incorporate (in varying degrees) elements of Hinduism, Buddhism, mysticism, and traditional religion (animism). The same is true of the village Muslim in India, Bangladesh, Pakistan, Malaysia, and Africa. In fact it is said that 70 percent of all Muslims have been influenced by folk, as opposed to orthodox, Islam.

Judaism also is a kaleidoscope of beliefs and practices, ranging from Orthodox to Conservative and from Reformed to Reconstructionist. Even more importantly, Judaism has been powerfully influenced by modern thinking. Many Jews in the West have adopted secularism. Although they remain Jews, their beliefs and practices are far removed from Old Testament revelation. They are, for all intents and purposes, outsiders; they are secularists.

Our inability to determine in the abstract whether Jews or Muslims experience insider or outsider conversion is not essential, because in both cases their beliefs are not isolated entities. Unlike the beliefs of most Westerners, Jewish and Muslim beliefs are so inextricably intertwined with their concepts of community, self-identity, and nationhood that Christian conversion is viewed not merely as a doctrine calling for belief but as an assault on that community, identity, and nationhood. Any discussion of the gospel's effects on Jews or Muslims must be considered within this framework.

Survival in Community

The history of the Jewish people is the story of survival. Although this was most poignant during the Nazis' attempted genocide of the Jews during World War II, the struggle has never been far from Jewish life or consciousness. As a minority in many "Christian" and Muslim lands, Jews were not given the status of "guests" but were considered "usable aliens." Consequently, they had a precarious existence. Until the eighteenth century, no country gave Jews equal protection under the law or considered them citizens. Therefore the Jews learned to survive as a minority. One of their most important survival skills was their ability to resist the attempts of the majority to convert them without incurring the majority's wrath. Jews used ridicule as a potent weapon of rejection. Derisive laughter, loaded with contempt but disguised as humor, is an effective way to deal with ideas one does not want to consider.

No Jew, however, would dare ridicule the priests' conversionist arguments, because priests often enjoyed the support of the secular authorities. There were even civil laws against blasphemy. Therefore, the rabbis devised several clever arguments to show that it was impossible for a Jew to believe in the tenets of the Christian religion. These arguments pitted the Jewish understanding of the Hebrew Scriptures against such cardinal Christian doctrines as the Trinity, the incarnation, substitutionary atonement, and the integrity of the New Testament. Christians who prepared careful expositions of these topics were sadly disappointed to find that the rabbis were totally unconvinced by their logical, well-documented answers. These scholars failed to understand that Jewish resistance to the gospel could not be overcome by demonstrating the veracity of these doctrines from Scripture. These Jews did, indeed, fulfill the Scriptures that described them as "stiff-necked" and as "hard-hearted."

There were not many formal disputes between Jews and Christians, even though each side maintained a carefully prepared arsenal of polemical arguments. Sometimes ecclesiastical decrees forced the Jews into formal debates, which were designed by the bishops to coerce Jewish leaders into admitting the truth of Christianity. As a means of self-preservation, Jews invariably kept to themselves. Indeed, the word *ghetto* first referred to concentrations of Jews living in European cities. This pattern emerged during the Middle Ages and has been preserved to this day. There has been a general expectation that people who live in the same place and who have the same nationality would share the same religion. This expectation has caused problems for other groups in Europe, not just for the Jews. In Poland,[1] the diversity of religious beliefs meant that many villages did not trade or communicate with each other. Most villages and towns were Roman Catholic, but near the eastern border many villages were Russian Orthodox, and toward the Prussian border some villages were Lutheran.

Even large cities were divided into districts where people lived among their coreligionists. Under Czarist law, different minorities were accorded different rights, but few had less rights than the Jews. Most of the large Russian cities were "off limits" to Jews. But the Jewish religion itself created a separation between Jews and non-Jews. For instance, Jewish law required Jews to live in a Jewish community (ten Jews were necessary for a minyan or prayer quorum), forbade them to travel beyond two thousand cubits on a Sabbath, and restricted the meat they ate to meat that had been slaughtered and sold by a kosher butcher. Regardless of whether the majority religion tried to exclude them or

1. Before the Holocaust, Poland had the largest Jewish population in Europe, approximately 3.5 million.

not, Jews still needed to form communities to meet certain requirements.

Although each Jewish community possessed a somewhat different culture that reflects its own history and experience, Jewish communities were held together by the Jewish religion and sense of identity. For these communities to be inclusive of Jews, they had to be exclusive of Gentiles. Nevertheless, the Jewish communities did absorb some culture from the surrounding communities. For example, Jews who were expelled from Spain and Portugal in 1492 moved to other Mediterranean countries, but they continued to speak an argot language called Ladino, which was derived from Spanish. Central and northern European Jews spoke a language called Yiddish, which was based on German. Jewish communities had different foods and folkways, and they celebrated Jewish holidays in different ways. Dissimilar marriage practices reflected the surrounding culture. Jews who lived in "Christian" lands practiced monogamy. Since there was no Talmudic prohibition against polygamy, Jews who lived among Muslims or Parsis allowed a man to have more than one wife.

To be a Jew involved living in a Jewish community. For Jews, it was inconceivable that a Jew could retain his or her religious identity outside of a Jewish community. Jewish fear of anti-Semitism (real and imagined) made the thought of life on the outside terrifying. Jewish knowledge of conversion was based on rabbinic requirements for Gentiles who converted to Judaism. Jews presumed that the same requirements would apply to Jews who converted to Christianity. Gentile conversion to Judaism required converts to renounce their former religion, family, and heritage and leave their people, just as Ruth left her family in Edom.

The rabbis of the Mishnaic and Talmudic times developed the procedures and regulations for conversion to Judaism.

For them, converting to Judaism did not mean discovering and finding a faith, as much as it meant initiation into a new community of a different religion. Conversion was a legal procedure; there was no principle of *sola fide*. The convert's relationship to God might have been a matter of faith, commitment, and conviction; but to the rabbis, it was a relationship to Israel that was carefully regulated by biblical and Jewish law. The Babylonian Talmud describes this conversion process:

> Our Rabbis taught: if at the present time a man desires to become a proselyte, he is to be addressed as follows: "What reasons have you for desiring to become a proselyte? Do you not know that Israel at the present time is persecuted and oppressed, despised, harassed, and overcome by afflictions?" If he replies, "I know and yet am unworthy," he is accepted forthwith, and is given instruction in some of the minor and some of the major commandments. He is informed of the sin [of the neglect of the commandments of] gleanings, the forgotten sheaf, the corner, and the poor man's tithe. He is also told of the punishment for the transgression of the commandments. Furthermore, he is addressed thus: "Be it known to you that before you came to this condition, if you had eaten suet you would not have been punishable with 'kareth' (excision or cutting off from the Jewish people); were you to profane the Sabbath you would not have been punishable with stoning; but now were you to eat suet you would be punishable with kareth; were you to profane the Sabbath you would be punishable with stoning."
>
> And as he is informed of the punishment for the transgression of the commandments, so is he informed of the reward granted for their fulfillment. He is told, "Be it known to you that the world to come was made only for the righteous, and that Israel for the present time are unable to bear either too much prosperity or too much suffering." He is not, however,

to be persuaded or dissuaded too much. If he accepted, he is circumcised forthwith. . . . As soon as he is healed arrangements are made for his ablution (baptism by immersion). At his ablution two learned men must stand by his side and acquaint him with some of the minor commandments and some of the major ones. When he comes up after his ablution he is deemed to be an Israelite in all respects.

In the case of a woman proselyte, women make her sit in the water up to her neck, while two learned men stand outside and give her instruction in some of the minor commandments and some of the major ones (47:a-b).

The references to the law of the sheaves and the poor man's tithe were meant to make the convert identify with the Book of Ruth and her statement to Naomi: "Your people shall be my people, and your God my God" (Ruth 1:16). This process of conversion might seem simple, but as far as Jewish law was concerned, it had many ramifications. In Israel today the validity of conversions made under non-Orthodox rabbis is hotly debated. A convert is certified to take his or her place in the Jewish community by meeting all of the requirements and having appropriate rabbis follow the traditional procedures. To become part of the community means that the converts renounce their affiliation with their family and nationality. This is the standard of the traditional, or Orthodox, rabbis. Conservative and Reformed Jews are somewhat more lenient.

Since proselytes to Judaism are required to forsake their families to become part of a new people, Jews might infer that converts to Christianity also must abandon and renounce the Jewish people. In fact in January 1978 the Knesset (Parliament of the State of Israel) passed a law making it a criminal offense for missionaries in Israel to give Jews money to convert to Christianity. Whether there had been any cause for this type of concern is doubtful. But this law does illustrate the

Knesset's misconception of the nature of evangelical conversion and reveals their fear that the nation might dwindle, in part through conversion. Plainly, the assumption is that a converted Jew is no longer a Jew.

In order to exclude the convert, some rabbis teach that the Jew who becomes a Christian must be regarded as a sinner and therefore must be shunned by his fellow Jews. The convert forfeits all the privileges of being Jewish and has no right to participate in Jewish community activities. Nevertheless, he still has all the obligations of being Jewish. Ironically, this adds to his burden of "sin," since he cannot fulfill these obligations. On one hand, the convert is excluded because he believes in Jesus; on the other hand, he is condemned by the rabbis for departing from the community. The convert finds himself in a "no win" situation.

The fear that Christian conversion violates the Jewish community coalesces with several other facts. First, Jews face the frustration of dwindling numbers. According to U. O. Schmelz and Sergio Della Pergola, the world's thirteen million Jews reached zero population growth in 1982. The chief problem is low fertility. In one case study, Britain's Jewish population dropped from 410,000 to 354,000 between the early 1960s and late 1970s. This has to be an alarming trend for a people who have survived, albeit painfully, for so long.

Second, intermarriage with non-Jews is becoming a global phenomenon. In Paris, which contains half of France's Jewish population, the rate of intermarriage is 50 percent. In the United States, Jewish intermarriage was at 32 percent in 1971. It rose to 40 percent in 1976, and it continues to rise. The Latin American Jewish intermarriage rate is even higher.

Third—and perhaps the most important cause for alarm— are the increasing problems of dissatisfaction and assimilation. Too many Jews do not live as Jews or relate to other Jews as coreligionists. According to Alfred Gottschalk, president of the Hebrew Union College Jewish Institute of Religion, "More than half the Jews in America play no part in Jewish communal life." This includes attending a synagogue or belonging to any Jewish organization.

From the Jewish perspective, religion is not a transcultural matter but an inextricable component in the way people view themselves, their family, community, and nation. The call to Christ is not just a call to accept him; it is a call to abandon Jewishness, to forsake one's family, and to desert one's nation. It is as mortal a threat as the one posed by the Nazis. Rabbis are fond of saying that there are two ways to exterminate a Jew: kill him or convert him.

There is a strikingly similar and comparable dynamic in Islamic communities. Although in Islamic communities the question of survival is not prominent and the history of Islam has been quite different from the history of Judaism, this dynamic becomes immediately apparent when a believer is baptized. Baptism is the decisive step of a believer's public self-identification with Christ, a step that marks his or her self-distinction from the unbelieving community. This change is subsequently evidenced by transformed standards of ethical conduct and lifestyle.

The Muslim community interprets this self-distinction not in moral and ethical terms but as a change of status. By rejecting Islam as the final and complete source of religious truth, the Christian takes himself or herself out of the community. Baptism symbolizes acceptance and appropriation of Christ's death and resurrection as the basis of salvation. Islam's law of apostasy states that such heretical action should result in death. At the very least, the Christian is cut off from the benefits of community life—access to financial, material, legal, social, and psychological support systems. In practical terms, the person is regarded as nonexistent or "dead." Sometimes a funeral service is even held.

Doctrine

Given the communal sense of Judaism and Islam, accepting the gospel will always mean a massive shift in social and cultural allegiance. It may be regarded as the extension of an alien culture, especially in the case of Muslims. In their minds, Christianity is identified with Western culture, colonial domination, exploitation, and imperialism. The moral decadence of the so-called Christian society in the West is rejected because it falls far short of Muslim piety.

Although Judaism and Islam are different belief systems, there are some interesting comparisons between the troubled Jewish Christian recipients of the book of Hebrews and modern Muslims.

The Jewish Christians addressed in the book of Hebrews had at least three important areas of misunderstanding about Christianity. Christologically, these Jews did not accept Jesus as the final and authoritative mediator of God's will. Apparently they continued to attach some importance to angels (Heb. 1:4–2:18) and to Moses (3:1–6) and to see them as competitors of the status and role they assigned to Jesus. Soteriologically, they did not completely accept the efficacy of Christ's sacrifice and the superiority of his mediatorial powers because they still recognized the Levitical priesthood and sacrificial ritual (4:14–5:11; 7:1–10:39). For them, salvation did not come by faith alone; they still valued ceremonial ablutions, the laying on of hands, and certain dietary regulations (6:1–2; 9:10, 14; 13:9). Ecclesiologically, these Jewish Christians withdrew from the wider Christian community because of some perceived incompatibility (probably a Gentile Christian minority, Heb. 13:17) and to avoid persecution (12:1ff.). These three misunderstandings were the result of the Jewish Christians' desire to bring certain Jewish beliefs and practices into Christianity. The writer of Hebrews urged them to a better understanding of the significance of Christ's person and work, to leave behind those rituals that had propped up their faith, and to make a distinct break with Judaism by clearly identifying themselves as part of the body of Christ.

There are some similarities between these early Jewish believers and today's Muslims, though there are important differences, too. Muslims who come to Christ bring certain concepts from Islam that do not need to be discarded but which should take on a deeper and fuller meaning. These elements of continuity include belief in the one true God, in angels, in prophets, in revealed Scripture (though this must be transferred to the Bible), in judgment, and in the sovereignty of God.

Other beliefs and practices are more questionable. These include the obligatory duties (din) of Islam: the confession of faith (Shahada: "there is no god but God, and Muhammad is the apostle of God"), prayers (salat), almsgiving (zakat), pilgrimage (Hajj), fasting (Ramadan), and striving (jihad). All of these have biblical counterparts (in fact for some of them the phrase *biblical origins* might be more correct). But the reason that Muslims perform these duties is fundamentally different from the reason given in the Bible. Christians perform spiritual deeds as a consequence or fruit of salvation. Muslims, however, perform good deeds to obtain merit before God. The Muslim hopes that good works will result in mercy and forgiveness and lead to salvation from hell. The Muslim believes these duties have soteriological significance and are not culturally conditioned expressions of faith.

In the light of this discussion, can converted Muslims adequately divorce these forms of religious observance from the meaning they formerly had in Islam? Isn't there the danger that continued use of these forms will hinder a correct understanding of the basis of the Christian faith, as was apparently the case in similar circumstances for the recipients of the book of Hebrews? The end result may be a group of people who are neither authentically Christian nor truly Muslim but somewhere in between. Sometimes it is assumed that the parallels between Islam, Christianity, and Judaism make the transition from the first to the second smoother than is the case with other religious traditions. The example of the recipients of the book of Hebrews teaches just the opposite. The greatest danger of incomplete and ultimately ineffectual conversion exists precisely where there is a high degree of continuity between Christianity and the religious tradition to which the convert formerly belonged.

This brings us to the third and most problematic category. This category centers around what is necessary for believing Christ's gospel. The difficulties arise from what the Reformers called the formal and material principles, authority and salvation.

First, Muslims consider the Bible to be corrupted and do not treat it as a source of truth. Instead, they believe in the divine origin of the Quran, which is therefore superior to all previous revelations, abrogating them where necessary. This applies especially to the Torah, Zabur, and Injil and to the Jewish and Christian Scriptures.

Second, Islam wrongly believes that the trinity is God, Jesus, and Mary. Therefore, Muslims reject the doctrine of the trinity as tritheism. Inevitably this means that the incarnation is seen as an impossibility. Indeed, the greatest sin in Islam is to associate another with God (shirk). Who, then, was Jesus? Jesus was a prophet, a worthy prophet, but one who was inferior to Muhammad.

Islam's denial of Christ's deity is linked to the negation of his work on the cross. Islam holds that Christ's substitutionary atonement was unnecessary on two counts. First, Islam has no concept of original sin. By nature human beings are good and only need guidance to know how to do what is right. Second, God forgives by decree. He forgives whom he wills and does not forgive whom he wills. Apart from these theological issues, the cross is unthinkable for a Muslim because God would never permit his prophet to be dishonored by crucifixion.

The two doctrinal stumbling blocks that stand between Muslims and the gospel are sin and Christ. Conviction of sin is outside the Muslims' normal experience and may not motivate them to turn to Christ. Muslims have no doctrine of original sin, and they teach that to a significant degree salvation depends on human effort. Muslim cultures are shame-oriented, not guilt-oriented. The highest value is the preservation of honor, particularly the honor of Allah. The motivation to seek forgiveness through good works is not to cover personal wrongdoing but to atone for dishonoring God's holiness.

Biblical faith requires everyone, no matter what the culture or religion, to believe that Jesus is the means and the way of submission (islam) to God. According to the Bible, Jesus is the God to whom we are to submit. No Muslim can have saving faith unless he or she sees Jesus in this light. Seeing Jesus in this way may require slightly different things for individual Muslims.

For the Sunni (orthodox) Muslim, Jesus must replace Muhammad as the acknowledged source of revealed truth for life and faith. This also entails an acceptance of the Bible in place of the Quran. For the Shi'ite Muslim, Jesus must replace Husayn as the ransom for his people and as the intercessor before God. For the Folk (syncretistic/animistic) Muslim, Jesus must be acknowledged as the power of God who effectively liberates humanity from the powers of evil or demonic activity. In this basically animistic worldview, demonic activity is not confined to the spiritual/psychological/mental sphere of human experience but also influences the physical and material world (through illness, accident, financial disaster, crop failure, natural calamity, etc.). For the Sufi (mystical) Muslim, Jesus must be recognized as the source of ultimate spiritual truth, as the only pathway to union with God, and as the means whereby we may experience the reality of God's love.

Some of the preceding remarks about Muslims could be made about Jews, though there are some obvious differences. In both cases, however, the gospel involves change. Both Muslims and Jews must acknowledge Jesus not only as a prophet but also as the promised Messiah, the one whose reign has already begun, as the only way to God the Father, and as the one who cancels our sin and who brings us into the worldwide family of those who have been renewed by God's Spirit. Only through Christ can anyone begin to live a new life of righteousness and love. Jews and Muslims each have their own special difficulties in seeing Christ in this way. But without belief in this gospel, there can be no acceptance with God.

Seeing Jesus as Messiah and sin-bearer and as Lord and master involves Jews and Muslims in an agonizing reappraisal that is not only religious but social, relational, and often financial. To be a believer and to declare this belief publicly by receiving baptism means rejecting family and nation. It means personal rejection and loss of housing, employment, and acceptance. It therefore seems inescapable that missionaries who take the gospel into these religions must accept certain responsibilities for their converts, who may, by their acceptance of the gospel, be left bereft and abandoned by all who have been close to them.

6

Religious Outsiders

Hindus and Buddhists

The ancient, highly developed religions of Hinduism and Buddhism do not lend themselves to easy analysis. This is partly due to their religious complexity; partly it is due to the fact that both have produced their respective cultures and cannot be understood apart from these cultures; partly it is due to the fact that both are based on a fuzzy-set mindset (meaning that clear distinctions are not seen as desirable, but rather that truth is a matter of a continuum); and finally, this is so because in both cases God or the Ultimate is beyond knowledge and definition. The gulf between these religions, on the one hand, and Christianity and Islam on the other, is very deep. It is also the case that East is East and West is West and the twain may meet, but only with great difficulty!

No Lines

We have already noted that Christian faith requires both bounded-set thinking and relational or centered-set thinking.

It operates with a clear sense of the distinction between right and wrong, truth and falsehood. Its gospel is presented as truths to which assent is asked. A gospel that lacks these truths—such as the incarnation of the Word, Christ's death in our place for our sin, our culpability before God for our sin, the meaning of his grace, and the place of faith—is not the biblical gospel. This, then, is a set of truths around which is a boundary, setting them off from ideas that are different. The gospel, however, is not just truths to be believed; it also concerns the Christ who must be acknowledged, believed, worshiped, and served. This is the gospel's center. Christian faith, therefore, calls for the sinner to come within the boundaries of truth and to submit himself or herself to the one who is the truth and thus to find a new allegiance. Thus the gospel is bounded and centered. In both Hinduism and Buddhism, however, the habits of thought are entirely different.

For the Hindu, religion is not a matter of accepting truths or even participating in rituals. It is, rather, the experience of reality (*anubhava*) that produces insight (*darsana*). Most Hindus recognize that Hinduism is not a dogmatic creed but a vast, complex, subtly unified mass of spiritual thought and realization. The great purpose of life is to strive to reach the Supreme. The paths to the Supreme, however, may well be different, for God is above the law, beyond the judgment he issues, and other than the love of which we know. Nevertheless, the Hindu really believes, in spite of proclamations to the contrary, that India is the source of wisdom, that all religions will ultimately discover the dharmic truth of Hinduism, that Krishna represents the total reality of the Supreme Brahmana. This, however, is perhaps the result of a new pride in India, for Hinduism itself is open to many different religious approaches to the Supreme. God is, in fact, beyond definition and no one can "reach" an understanding of the inexhaustible being of God or experience the infinite number of its expressions in the short span of one human life.

Most Hindus may be willing to accept the divinity of Christ, but they deny his uniqueness. He may be one of the ways to God, but he is not the only way. Hindus can accept the idea that Christ was a manifestation of God, and the fact that he was also human is attractive. But that he was uniquely the incarnation of God and uniquely bore our sin is offensive to Hindus.

Because Hindus believe that God is manifested in myriads of ways, they are willing to talk about and even experience Christ as one of those ways. They are not willing to foreclose on the others, however. And because they regard religion as a lifelong search, Hindus resist making immediate decisions, especially ones of eternal importance. There is a deep sense of the mystery and vastness of the thing being contemplated. To make a decision about the nature of reality or about Christ in a short time is to assume that more is known and has been experienced than is actually possible. This action is therefore arrogant and ignorant.

The theistic base of Buddhism is even more obscure; indeed, by some definitions, Buddhism is atheistic. Buddhists see "conversion" not as a turning from sin *to God*, but as an emancipation from the self and, correspondingly, from the illusion of the world around. What one is freed *for* is beyond words and definitions. Indeed, the very desire for words and definitions—bounded or even centered-set thinking—is itself evidence of bondage to illusion and of the absence of enlightenment.

Zen Buddhism illustrates this type of thinking. In this form of Buddhism, the equivalent of Christian conversion, though it is also quite different, is enlightenment. Enlightenment means an alteration in the self's attitude toward the world and a transformation of consciousness. This results in a radical attempt to overcome the subject-object scheme (a person's sense of the world being the subjective element and the world itself being the objective) in order to achieve a genuine self-transcendence. But what is self-transcendence, and how might it be achieved?

One of the central practices in Eastern religions is meditation (*dhyana*), which aims to develop a person's ability to concentrate and thus to still the mind. Through a deep stage of concentration, the mind is unified and transcends the subject-object structure of the intellect; thus self-transcendence is realized. However, we can distinguish two approaches to the process of meditation. In the first approach, a person concentrates on a special word or image, usually with the help of a correct physical posture and the control of breathing, to evoke a sense of tranquility and release. But there is another approach, called *zazen* by the Zen Buddhists. The uniqueness of *zazen* is that the mind becomes completely empty. Without this evacuation, the person is not able to rise above his or her own particular existence and see things as they really are. Such a stage of concentration is, of course, more transcendent than the former one because it achieves a genuine dissolution of the split between subjectivity and objectivity, between the context of the person's mind and the outside world.

The Rinzai sect of Zen Buddhism suggests an even more radical way of attaining self-transcendence. If transcendence is a complete liberation from subjectivity and objectivity, Rinzai Zen argues that even *zazen* ("without-thinking") is inadequate. For if the attainment of self-transcendence is limited to *zazen*, there is still a cleavage between one's ordinary life and life in *zazen*. Such a withdrawal and separation from everyday life cannot be regarded as the supreme stage of self-transcendence. A supreme stage of self-transcendence must be realized in an *ordinary* life, yet at the same time maintain a state of mind that overcomes the dichotomy between subjectivity and objectivity. The goal is an island of tranquility within, the Calm Self, even when the edges of the shore are being battered by the demands and activities of life. This goes far beyond simply having "a sense of peace." It requires a disengagement from life, from one's own thoughts about the past, present, and future, even while one functions in the midst of life. This self-transcendence is a state of "no-mindedness." It is the realization of inner dislocation from the world, of hearing but not hearing, of living in the world but not being part of it, of knowing the world and yet not letting it occupy one's thoughts.

There is a Japanese story about two Zen Buddhist monks who come to a stream and find a beautiful woman waiting to be helped across. One monk, remembering the regulations that forbid physical contact with a woman, refuses to help her. The other picks her up and carries her across the stream. Some time later, after the monks resume their journey, the first one upbraids the second for his action. The second responds that he put the woman down as soon as they crossed the stream, whereas the first monk has ever since carried her in his mind! Enlightenment, then, is nonattachment to things and experiences, disengagement from thought, and emancipation from experience.

Buddhists believe that behind the world we know, behind the particulars of what we experience, is the Buddha-nature (*bussho*). At the same time the nature is latent or immanent in all living beings, who therefore contain and point toward this Buddha nature. Because people distinguish themselves from everything else and have an individual sense of self-consciousness, they are blind to this reality. The aim therefore is to be awakened to the nature of this kindness. It is to understand our bondage due to our individuality. It is to establish a merging into the ultimate quietness of nonbeing.

Cultures built around the belief that all creatures share the Buddha-nature have distinctive forms. The style of Japanese art, for example, with its imbalance, asymmetry, simplification, and above all, radical creativity, characterizes the emphasis of informality, antidogmatism, and the breakthrough of the subject-object scheme in Zen enlightenment. Another peculiar feature of Japanese culture is the art of tea (*chanoyu*). Serving tea in a tearoom (or, tea-ceremony) is a way to transcend a person's consciousness and pass into an intensive stage of concentration. The main emphasis during the ceremony is, again, *simplification*, the elimination of the unnecessary. And such ideas of simplification and elimination once again also remind us of the pursuit of concentration and tranquility in Zen. There is also a close relationship between Zen and the Japanese view of nature. The ontological grounding of the Japanese culture's intensive love of nature can be traced back to the belief in the Buddha-nature. The radically immanent conception of Buddha-nature imparts a strong sense of *identification* between humans and nature. We can take the Japanese style of architecture as an example. Not only the building materials (usually bamboo and wood), but also the architectural design of the buildings and gardens reveal an attempt at harmonization between people and nature. A Japanese hut is designed to be in harmony with nature so that the person who lives in it simply becomes another part of nature, taking his or her place among the birds, flowers, insects, and stream.

The basic philosophy underlying Japanese *Bushido* (the way of the warrior) and swordsmanship is a person's absolute loyalty and view of death. The *samurai's* (warrior's) view that "living is dying and dying is living" presents a Zen ideal of *nonattachment*. The *samurai* is not attached to his life; it is of no consequence to him and so he is ready to yield it.

The Face-Off

The propagation of the Christian gospel in India and Japan, for example, is hindered by many obstacles, the most immediate of which is cultural. Religion has embodied itself in the cultures and the people in those cultures equate being Indian and Japanese with their respective religions. Christian faith is therefore seen not only as a different faith, but as the intrusion of an alien culture. Christianity is Western. The gospel may be seen as an arm of imperialism or colonialism (although this is more likely in India than in Japan).

This difficulty has been exacerbated, especially in India, by the consequences that have followed for believers. Converted Hindus, especially if they come from upper social classes, are rejected by their families. They also are socially ostracized. To compensate for their rejection, these converts often adopt new lifestyles, new value systems, and Western culture. The process, though perfectly understandable, makes Christians look like aliens within their Indian culture. In the minds of most Indians, the gospel thus becomes even more westernized.

Because of the social condemnation that invariably follows, a Hindu often hesitates to declare belief in Jesus Christ. This is especially true if the person is from an upper-caste background. Converts are made to feel like traitors to the Indian cause and are considered a disgrace to their families. The whole family—and family ties are very strong in India—feels ashamed of the person who claims to be a Christian.

At least until recently, a majority of Christian converts in India came from lower Hindu castes. These new Christians adopted a unique blend of Western and Indian cultural life-styles. Upper-caste Hindus never fully accepted these new converts as social equals. Because Western missionaries in India were reluctant to take a stand on cultural issues, Christianity continued to be associated with this particular culture.

An upper-caste Hindu, even though he or she is convinced of Jesus's claims, faces a tremendous cultural dilemma. Such a person may want to accept Christ, but may not want to be associated with the Christian lifestyle in India. People like this do not want to give up their culture, their values, their Indianness. However, when they do turn to Christ, they find themselves surrounded by other Indian Christians who do not, in a real sense, speak their language.

This problem is compounded by the different styles of thought in Hinduism, Buddhism, and Christianity. The gospel has been presented as truths to be believed, not as mysteries in which seekers can lose themselves. The gospel forecloses endless discovery and searching; it announces that it is the end of the quest. To both the Hindu and the Buddhist this sounds profoundly wrong-headed, for both are embarked upon roads whose destination is far, far away; the truth is not at hand. Both believe that the gospel stated as the truth and stated in propositions to be believed shows how mistaken it is. Both are deeply opposed to the "dogmatism" of exclusive belief; Buddhists especially oppose anchoring that truth in words, for words belong in the world of illusion. Thus the cultures, the social norms, the habits of thought become hard, protective, and almost impenetrable casings.

This surely is a powerful reminder of the truth of Paul's exposition in Ephesians 2:1–10, in which he develops the interconnections between the world, the flesh, and the devil. We all, he says, "followed the ways of this world" (2:2); we all followed the norms and customs of our respective cultures, each of which, in different ways, makes sin and rebellion against God look normal. Why is this? Because, Paul tells us, there is a pervasive relationship between culture and "the prince of the power of the air" (2:2), who works "in the sons of disobedience" (2:2). We need to see, then, that the cultural obstacles to the gospel are ultimately demonic obstacles to the kingdom of God. Before conversion, Paul said, all of us lived by these influences. They gave us permission to gratify our fallenness and to show who we really are. It is no surprise to learn that, outside of Christ, "we were by nature children of wrath" (2:3).

This interconnection is the key, it would seem, to evangelism in these cultures. For if the cultures themselves are like great barrier reefs that protect those on the shores, the most effective evangelists will be those already in the cultures. In India, they will be Indians who are not westernized, but whose stories, testimonies, songs, worship services, and prayers bear the imprint of Indian sociocultural heritage without, of course, even a whisper of Hinduism. They will be people who live authentically Christian lives, for Indians expect "holy" people who hold public discourses on religion to be holy, to exhibit purity and piety. And they will be people who will not be afraid to enter into the kinds of conversations where deep, probing questions are asked. In both Buddhism and Hinduism, this is how religious truth is found. The Western evangelical habit of foreclosing on discussion and thought on the grounds that all the truth anyone really needs is contained in a simple rendition of the gospel is profoundly unsatisfactory to Hindus and Buddhists.

There are significant ethical responsibilities attendant upon taking the gospel into cultures where those who believe will, in all likelihood, be dispossessed by their families and perhaps by employers and landlords as well. Where will such a person find the spiritual and psychological help as well as the material assistance to survive if not in the Christian community? In these cultures the gospel has to be a call to come to Christ, and an invitation to join the Christian community, the church.

This is the context in which profoundly different understandings of God can be addressed. For there are not many roads to him, but one. He is not mystery; because we are made in his image we can receive his disclosure of himself that he has given us in the words of Scripture. We *can* know him. He is not underlying all living beings, although he gives life to everything. We are separated from him by sin; our self-centeredness has to be put to death in Christ, but that is not the same thing as putting to death our self-consciousness. Indeed, God has so disclosed himself that in knowing him through Christ and Scripture, we can begin to live in his world on his terms with joy, not merging ourselves into him but knowing that we are creatures before the Creator, not moving toward self-extinction but toward the affirmation of our dependence on him as a result of which our individual personalities are redeemed for his service. We do not negate this world but recognize it as God's and seek to bring it, with all of its wealth and beauty, to him through Christ our Lord. This is the joyful affirmation that can and must be made in ways indigenous to these cultures. May it be done more and more!

7

Materialistic Outsiders

Materialism is the view that there is nothing but matter: there is no spiritual dimension, no moral world, no supernatural, and no God. Materialists are therefore opposed to idealists, who think that reality is ideas, and to any understanding of the world that sees in it a spiritual dimension.

But materialists are of two kinds. Some, like the Marxists, are philosophical; others, like most Westerners, are unthinking. Marxists are theoretical atheists whereas secular Westerners are practical atheists. For them, materialism is not a system of thought that has inclined them to exclude God from consideration but a whole web of relationships in life whose interests are centrally affluent and whose cognitive horizons make the pursuit of "the good life" normative.

Secularism, which leads to materialism, is the assumption that the processes of life are separated from any divine or moral order standing behind them. God may indeed exist—and few Westerners doubt that he does—but his existence is not meaningful to any part of life. To say that he exists is to say nothing concrete about whether there are enduring values, an ultimate distinction between right and wrong, what life is about, what its meaning is, and why one wants to live it. Affirming God means little, denying him means little; understanding life on its own terms is everything.

If we do not, or cannot, anchor meaning in God because he is too distant, indistinct, and disconnected from our lives, then we have no alternative but to find meaning in ourselves. What is right and wrong, true and false, important and trivial, is derived from our experience. Experience becomes a teacher who both serves up what values there are and corrects us in terms of those values. So pluralism has become an inescapable part of modern reality. Who is to say that one value is preferable to another? If experience is the criterion, the quarry out of which we dig meaning, then whatever seems to "fit" for each individual should be accepted, at least for the moment.

It should not surprise us that forms of Eastern thought, especially Hinduism, have found such a happy reception in the West, or that Western secularism, like the AIDS virus, has traveled all over the world and found lodging even in some contexts that have been deeply religious. Common to Western and Eastern worldviews today is the idea that life is just a mass of unrelated, fast-moving, separate experiences, many of which may be running counter to one another. The resolution to this experiential ambiguity in the East is found beyond the natural; in the West it is found within the natural. The mysticism of Eastern thought is more externally focused, that of Western thought more internally focused.

As a result, Western culture has accepted that it is only in the self—its needs, feelings, and desires—that we have access to meanings. The world above is gone; only the world within remains. The world within, however, is murky and indistinct. It is confused and hard to understand. It is contradictory and misleading. Ultimately, then, we come back to the proposition that there are probably many different kinds of experience that have ultimate meaning, that for the people involved they had validity, and therefore a person who claims a conversion experience is as right as someone who insists that he or she does not want such an experience.

This pluralism, and its parent secularism, are today undergirded in the West by powerful social forces that almost require those habits of mind. It is not difficult to see how secularization (the shape of modern society brought about principally by industrialization and urbanization) coalesces into secularism (values that result from disconnecting life from an overarching divine order). Consider, for example, the effect of cities.

In the Third World, one can find cities in which there are millions who are poor, young, homeless, and unemployed. These cities are often the congregating places for the afflicted, the dispossessed, and the disinherited, and no doubt their presence affects the character of the city. In the West, cities are different. They have their poor and unemployed but their numbers are by comparison far smaller. Western cities are also more technologically oriented. They are great centers of manufacture and commerce in which the pattern of people's lives has been shaped to meet the needs of producing goods and services.

The most important development here has been the sundering of private from public life. It used to be that the cobbler was someone who was known, not only for his work, but also for his character. In those days, personal reputation was prized. It was the social reward for the careful exercise of responsibility. Today, this relationship has been broken, for cities require most people to travel to work and thus to live in two worlds: their domestic world and their economic world. Few people, if any, know both of the worlds that an individual inhabits.

The economic world, furthermore, defines people by their *function*: it thinks of value, even the value of human beings, in terms of economic productivity. It is an impersonal world, where values are pragmatic and fluid. In this world, character is subjugated to productivity, ethics to performance, what is right to what produces the heftiest bottom line. There is economic accountability but little moral accountability.

This situation is not, of course, without its ironies, especially in the United States. Americans by every reckoning see themselves as religious, yet largely act as if God were not there; they are appalled by the atheism of Communist regimes, but practice atheism in public life and have to contend with the American Civil Liberties Union if they even want to display religious symbols on public property. People in the United States are horrified by the one-dimensional perspective of Marxist materialism but by an entirely different route are practicing their own one-dimensional materialism. It is true that Marxist regimes have systematically destroyed the freedoms central to the functioning of any democracy, freedoms that have been successfully preserved in America. But it is surely ironic that deeply materialistic Americans should construct a foreign policy designed to contain and even eliminate the other materialists in the world! It is especially ironic because the freedoms cherished by Americans are not derived from the materialistic worldview. The major reason America has fared as well as it has, it has been argued, is that it is now facing off against a foe who is weakened internally and whose own worldview is in disarray.

The practical materialism of the West and the theoretical materialism of Marxism are so close to one another that they can be bracketed here for consideration, even though most

Americans would be horrified to find themselves linked with Marxists! What we need to ask now is how the Christian teaching on conversion compares with, and can be presented to, people in this category.

Learning by Stages

Western secularism is producing a culture that is increasingly at odds with the Judeo-Christian worldview from which it arose. What one could assume the average person would know, think, and believe three decades ago can no longer be assumed. As a matter of fact, the West has now become sufficiently alienated from Christian values that Christians must engage in cross-cultural communication.

Evangelism in the West, however, commonly assumes that the simple presentation of the gospel message—perhaps the simpler the better—will create the least hindrance to the acceptance of Christian faith and that God will miraculously provide whatever other understanding is needed. This approach would be frowned upon on the mission field—and rightly so—but it is singularly inappropriate in the West as well. It appeals to our swift, technological, fix-it age: in no time at all, millions can be claimed to have been "reached" with the gospel. But beaming simple gospel truths at the masses is not the same as "reaching" them. We cannot claim that Christian faith has been communicated until it has been understood, and most secular people are no longer in a position to understand Christian truth if they hear only a minimal, packaged version of the gospel and are asked for immediate assent.

A majority of people today has little knowledge of Christianity and has few of the assumptions that go with it. They do not assume that God is meaningfully related to life and that making him the center and focus is the key to finding meaning; that there is an ultimate distinction between right and wrong; that human beings are not just chemicals and electrical charges but are made with a capacity for relations human and divine; that they are spiritual beings. People like this come to faith in stages. Their turning away from their former allegiance, such as the good life, to Christ may be protracted. It may climax in a dramatic "Damascus road" experience, but it is preceded by internal rearrangements and incrementally built knowledge of what the new alliance is and will entail.

This decision, in other words, falls within the pattern that functions with respect to any major decision that has significant implications. This "extended problem solving" has clearly discernible stages: a need is felt; there is a search for information; information produces alternatives that are then evaluated; a course of action is chosen and acted upon; after the commitment, reevaluation continues as the original need is placed alongside the solution adopted. This same process goes on in Christian conversion. However, this process needs to be clarified.

First, people do not decide for Christ in the same way that they purchase a house. In both cases the same process is operative, from need through alternatives to a solution. Purchasing a house, however, does not involve a change of allegiance; coming into relationship with Christ does. The gospel therefore cannot legitimately be packaged and sold like a product. The gospel does, in the deepest sense, meet human need, but the sinner is not a consumer. Any offer of the gospel that does not make plain the need for complete submission and unqualified allegiance to Christ is not biblical.

Second, the person's need must be interpreted. People may experience alienation within themselves and in their relationships, but they do not always realize that they are separated from God by their sin and that their problem stems from their alienation from God. Sin is a theological concept, and a reality to be defined in relation to God. We are sinners because we have rebelled against God, abandoned his truth, refused his law, defied his Christ, and placed ourselves in our Creator's place. We have become our own law, truth, and christ. Sin is not primarily about breaking rules, although it results in that; it is not at bottom about self-centeredness, although it always is that. It is at bottom a refusal to let God be God over life, to give him the center, the focus, the glory that are his. And every felt need must be understood in this light. Unless this is the case, we will go on producing grotesque aberrations such as the "health and wealth gospel," which links the "need" to be healthy and wealthy to the solution, a gospel that offers health and wealth.

Third, the solution (the gospel) will not be effectively embraced unless it does correlate with need. There may be "decisions," but these will be superficial and cursory. The need, however, that the gospel actually addresses is not necessarily the one that people feel. In one study, American university students identified material success as their greatest felt need. They considered material success to be fundamental to happiness. The need was happiness; the proposed path to it was affluence. The temptation then, is to market the gospel as the best means to happiness, because it meets the need and is somewhat true. However, a whole intermediate stage has been bypassed. The gospel promises acceptance with God and righteousness, not happiness, to repentant sinners. The concern of the New Testament is moral; today the concern is psychological. The desire for happiness is not in itself wrong, but if we are biblically disciplined, it will be a secondary concern. The moral relationship to God must be brought into focus; when this is rightly established in Christ, happiness may well be one of its consequences. At the same time, however, to offer repentance to someone looking for happiness is too abrupt. The long-term strategy is to find a way to enable the person who is looking for happiness to understand that the goal can be realized only through the process of repentance and a change of allegiance from the self, and its appetites for affluence, to Christ. This is a process, not something that can be accomplished in a single moment. And unless we have the patience to work within the process, the actual needs of the person will not be addressed. If Christ is seen to be the answer to the needs as the person has defined them, it may not be the biblical Christ to whom that person is responding.

Finally, most Western secularists have not even begun the extended process of decision making. Their needs are often confused and inchoate; they cannot interpret them because they have no idea whether God can be found or whether truth, right, and wrong exist. To present the gospel before explaining these basic elements is to assemble the roof before laying the foundation. The impatience of evangelicals in this matter, the feeling that somehow the "gospel is not being preached" when the preliminary work is being done, has produced guilt that has crippled such work. We need much more preparation, not less!

The Lonely Crowd

These points now need to be brought more fully into relation with Western society as we know it. What is this world like?

This world, as we have noted, is secularized. This does not mean that people are less religious; they might even be more interested in spiritual seeking than ever. It does mean that the institutions of society lose their sacral status. In other words, we no longer have a common agreement as to what is holy. The courts, the parliament, the schools, the government, and the hospitals no longer legitimate their existence by public contract about what is to be considered as holy. We are so familiar with this that it seems natural to us. This is one of the blind spots in our society. It is difficult to analyze things that are too close. But if we examine a system that differs greatly from the one we live in, light falls on our own circumstances.

Medieval society in Europe knew nothing about secularization. Everything in the medieval world was integrated in a meaningful "holy order," a hierarchical and complicated system that could be likened to a beautiful crystal chandelier. Everything was subordinated to the whole; individuals, in our definition of the word, did not exist. Time was cyclical, not linear. The cycle of seasons and the regular holy days of the church year structured everyday life. The heart of this society was the cathedral, where the holiest of all that is holy was administered. The miracle of incarnation occurred in the mass, the presence of God in bread and wine. From the cathedral holiness radiated out to all areas of social life—art, science, business, family. In a medieval town the market was situated immediately outside the cathedral. The things sold in the market had been made in the surrounding streets (hence such names as Baker Street and Potters' Lane).

People seldom chose their work; they inherited it from the family. The gift of marriage was more important than the individual who entered into it. Both in work and in family life the task was to act well in a given role. This sharply contrasts with our goal of "realizing ourselves" or being "fulfilled." In medieval society expansion, progress, and evolution were not the key words. The objective was not to teach a future goal but to reflect as truly as possible a heavenly pattern, a divine reality. In Dante's description of this society (*Paradiso*), nobody was trying to reach for a better or higher position. Every small detail of the whole was infinitely meaningful, and people rejoiced in that fact. That was freedom, said Dante. The Renaissance and the Reformation challenged the central position of the Catholic cathedral; modern thinking has challenged the centrality of God. The whole hierarchical system of the Middle Ages has broken down. Human beings stand alone before God, without the institutions that formerly protected them. This led to anguish in the seventeenth century, to a growing concept of the rights of individuals in the eighteenth century, and to political struggle for these rights in the nineteenth century.

In the twentieth century the Renaissance view of time, the human being, and history reached its peak in the conviction that history brings unbroken progress for mankind. But today, at the end of the century, this conviction is disintegrating. People are turning inward instead. When neither the past nor the present seems meaningful, what content remains in life? It seems only the subjective experiences of the mind are left. The individual disappears, even dissolves, without entering into a meaningful context, as was the case in the Middle Ages.

Something also happened to the concept of "holiness" during this passage of the centuries. The European history of thought, with its stress on the individual, has defined holiness as an *inner* quality; conversion becomes a turning of the individual toward pious acts, a fixed list of "signs of holiness." By contrast, the biblical concept of holiness means being set aside for another owner, belonging to someone else. If something is holy, it is out of the market; it is *not for sale.*

Since our society lacks common agreement about what is and is not holy, we are left with the conclusion that nothing is holy. Everything is for sale. The transplant industry wants our bodies; the cosmetic and genetic industries want our unborn babies. The tropical forests are for sale. Wars, some of which have already lasted longer than the Second World War, go on, and the weapons market flourishes as a result. That the cathedral in a European city or the church in the center of a New England town is not "useful" for any purpose other than worship is powerfully symbolic. The architectural language proclaimed forcefully the centrality and the freedom of grace—that it was not for sale and could not be bought. To worship is to be liberated from the merciless markets of life, to declare by God's grace that one is not for sale. It is to be for God, for his use and service, to be set free to marvel at his astonishing greatness and glory. This is the liberation, the marvel, toward which we must work as we encounter the naked, lonely men and women of the twentieth century who have only themselves to converse with in the desolate spaces of their inner life.

Modernity and secularism, in stripping life of its mystery and meaning, also have made us invisible to one another. Toward the end of the twentieth century we have seen a new person arise: the narcissistic person who has become his or her own world, is self-enclosed, and neither dares nor desires to escape the confinement of the inner domain. The outside world does not really interest the narcissistic person.

For the autistic person the outsider does not exist. Only inner experience counts; the world has no objective, real existence of its own. It is not possible to know anything about the world; no dialogue can be had with it; it cannot speak or act. When the autistic person stands by the sea, he or she does not encounter the sea, but simply the experience of the sea. If this person were in a sinking ship, he or she would be more interested in experiencing the catastrophe than in seeking a way to escape it.

Something in this total isolation and alienation is reminiscent of classical paintings of hell that depict a crowd of tormented people, seemingly together, but actually terribly alone, enclosed in their own pain and fear and unable to feel the others' distress. Who can rescue us from this chill of death, this ignorance that eats one more part of us every day, while we are flooded by a stream of real and artificial violence on the radio, on television, in the newspapers, in our homes, in our nightly fantasies? And at the same time we are offered more and more colorful "experiences" in food, clothes, journeys, sex, sport, culture, and religion.

"Among you stands one whom you do not know." John the Baptist was speaking. His voice comes to us from outside, far beyond ourselves, before us both in time and in space. His words are written down in a book that is not primarily an experience but a book about a factual, measurable, objective existence.

"Among you stands one whom you do not know." John spoke about Jesus. In the so-called Christian countries, we take for granted that if we know anything at all, we do at least know who Jesus is. His picture is torn and pale from centuries of intimacy; the colors have flaked off the figure until it has become white and harmless as Thorvaldsen's Christ—a bandage that covers reality.

Can we add anything to all the books that have been written about him, all the institutions and companies that have made use of his name? There may not be much to add, but there is much that needs to be stripped away! Christ is not an agitator. He offers no new, intense experiences. He does not sell anything. He *is*, and that is all—like a flower on the restaurant table in the midst of the smoke and the talk. This is not what everybody else is promising today. In the advertisements, in the porno papers, in the new spiritual movements the message is clear—we have exactly what you have been looking for! Here is the answer to all your questions! We'll straighten out the mystery of life for you! This simplification turns everyone into nothing more than a shallow consumer. Christ is not for consumption but for worship.

The person who knows God as Another—the one who is the Outside, whom we meet not as one of our experiences but as other than our experiences—is the person who can begin to see other people as well. When we have broken through the unreality that enables us to think that what is real is only what goes on in the inner recesses of our selves, we are in a position to see that others also have reality, that they are other than ourselves, that as we worship God so we can now love them.

Conversion has so often been understood as a narrow transaction that is religious but somehow not human, that does something in the soul but does not really involve the senses, one's laughter, one's will, where one wants to go, what one thinks about. This is what sociologists have in mind by their talk of the sundering of the private from the public. It is the twisting of faith that inevitably happens when people back into faith instead of building into it. The Bible, after all, does not begin with John 3:16; it begins with Genesis so that we might first understand who God is, who we are, what his creation is like, why we are in it, and what the end of this will be. To understand all of this and to be converted is to have what is needed to be a *human* who knows God; to have the gospel shorn of its biblical framework is to have a shard of religiousness that scarcely can penetrate all of the corners of one's humanity.

There is a story told in the Chassidic tradition about the rabbi of Rhizyn who was visited by men from the city of Sanok. They complained that while they scrupulously followed the rules, praying at dawn and then learning a chapter of

Mishna, the Chasidim were less careful in their observance of the law. The Chasidim did not always pray at dawn, and when they had finished they sat around drinking schnapps. What perturbed the men from Sanok was that the Chasidim were judged to be pious whereas they were called "the adversaries"!

The rabbi of Rhizyn explain that the Chasidim's behavior was really a device to trick the devil. After the set time of prayer, they sat down and drank together. "To life!" Each would tell what was burdening his heart and then they would say to one another, "May God grant your desire!" Since prayer can be offered in any language, they saw this also as prayer. The devil, on the other hand, only saw a group of people sitting around, drinking schnapps, and using everyday speech, and so he left them alone!

This, of course, is a joke. But it does illustrate how being religious and being human really should be connected and connected in such a way that the humanness is enriched by the religiousness and is put in its service.

Thus when we encounter secularists, lonely people for whom affluence and the senses are all that is left, we have to have in mind the biblical mandate: to bring them into sufficient knowledge of God, his world, his Christ, his law, and his truth that they turn to him in humble submission; to bring them out of the shadows of their self-enclosed worlds to see others; and to bring them from being invisible to having a full humanity that restores this part of the creation to something closer to the Creator's original intent. Although that is the objective, only the creator-redeemer God can accomplish it.

Marxism

From the vantage point of North American Christianity, the study of Marxism may appear as an esoteric and irrelevant occupation. It is a fact, though, that one-third of humanity lives in nations where Marxism is the established ideology. Millions encounter it on a day-to-day basis. Even when one is inclined to think that establishment tends to be the beginning of the end of any given ideology, the assessment recently given by Milovan Djilas, Yugoslavia's most prominent Marxist dissident, remains true: Marxism in the Soviet Union may be dead at the level of faith for most people but it is very much alive at the level of policy. Marxism, however, means more than a rationale of power in many situations around the world, especially in developing countries. In these countries, it is still a competing ideology, sometimes the only offer of a blueprint for comprehensive change of the social conditions that cry out for change. Marxism is then seen as a convincing analysis and synthesis of true human existence beyond its present alienations.

The Marxist Agenda

It is appropriate to investigate the Christian concept of conversion in the light of Marxism, because like Christianity, Marxism teaches that people need to undergo a radical change. Moreover, its concept of transformation is comparable to the Christian notion. Contrary to common misconception, Marxists postulate not only a change in social structures, but also a complementary change in the lives of individual human beings who populate these structures.

The need for such a change can be specified by pointing to the earlier extant piece of Karl Marx's writings, that is, the matriculation essay in religion that he wrote as a seventeen-year-old student. After surveying both the history of mankind and the development of individuals, he concluded that man is "the only being in nature which does not fulfill its purpose." Marx observed in man "a passion for what is good, . . . a yearning for truth, . . . enthusiasm for virtue." But "the sparks of the eternal are extinguished by the sweetly flattering power of lies." Humanity's deepest moral problem is "an unbridled egoism."

This moral problem also looms large in Marx's earliest statements from a Communist viewpoint, statements that at the same time further clarify not only the necessity but also the nature of the change that is needed. Looking at the external, political, constitutional liberation achieved by the French Revolution of 1789, Marx wrote of the task of "*changing*, so to speak, *human nature*." Quoting from Jean Jacques Rousseau, Marx defined the nature of this change as "*transforming* each individual, who in himself is a . . . solitary whole, into a *part* of a greater whole." He summed up in his own words: "Only when the real, individual man . . . as an individual human being has become a *species-being* [a social being] in his everyday life, in his particular work, and in his particular situation . . . , only then will human emancipation have been accomplished."

Thus, according to Marx, it is necessary to go beyond changes in structures and constitutions to help individuals become socially responsible and committed *citoyens*, instead of self-content and egoistic *bourgeois*. Communion clearly means not only the associated (instead of anarchic) form of production, but also the socialization of the whole of human existence. Communism advocates a change of attitude and behavior, a mutation not only in terms of "Economic Man," but also of a far more basic anthropological configuration.

Marx's specifications, together with his formula for change, explain his concern for "real humanism." His goal was not correction merely of title, name, or theory of consciousness, but of the practical reality of the work and the concrete relationships of the individual. This bottom line of *solidarity in practice* Marx and Engels consolidated in the ensuing debates with their previous colleague, Bruno Bauer. Marxism demands palpable changes. Marx summed up his interaction with his philosophical predecessor, Ludwig Feuerbach, by saying: "The philosophers have only *interpreted* the world in various ways; the point is to *change* it."

This call for "new men" has echoes in the history of Marxism-Leninism whenever a new generation dreams of a Communist utopia of truly unselfish people. It dominated the ideological debates in the Soviet Union of the 1960s. However, even in the decidedly more pragmatic utterances from the contemporary Soviet Union and mainland China, the theme is discernible. This can be shown from two documents generated in 1986: the *Political Report of the Central Committee to the Twenty-Seventh Party Congress* (plus the *Resolution of the Twenty-Seventh Congress*) and the *Resolution of the Central Committee of the Communist Party of China on the Guiding Principles of Building a Socialist Society with an Advanced Culture and Ideology* (September 1986).

The main theme of Mikhail Gorbachev's report was "the acceleration of the socioeconomic development." The emphasis is on modernization, that is, on new methods of management of economics, not on the "new type of man." Correspondingly, Gorbachev seemed to be somewhat wary of the insistence on ideological incentives. He thought that dwellings, food supplies, the quality of consumer goods, and the level of health care "must directly affect the consciousness and sentiment of the people."

Gorbachev is nevertheless fully aware of the changes this program demands in terms of people's attitude and behavior, what has been called the "psychological" aspect of the production process. He has said that "any of our plans would hang in the air if people are left indifferent." Therefore, the basic need is for a "social and spiritual emancipation of man. Nothing but this can make him truly free." Correspondingly, Gorbachev is involved in a running polemic against the inertia and hypocrisy of some of the party functionaries who are in charge of the economy. He believes that too few of them practice what they preach; too many lack the "unity of words and deeds" by which they are being judged. This is extremely dangerous, for it robs the Party of its credibility and annihilates the attractiveness of socialism as a real humanism. But "the Party's moral health is the earnest of society's health"; therefore, it must struggle for honesty, truth, and nothing but the truth, and replace the frequently encountered window dressing with a spirit of sober self-criticism. Otherwise, the Communist Party cannot be the "political and moral vanguard" of the nation.

The Chinese *Resolution on the Guiding Principles for Building a Socialist Society with an Advanced Culture and Ideology* reveals a train of thought that is not dissimilar to the one just described. Compared with the *Political Report and Resolution of the Twenty-Seventh Congress of the Soviet Communist Party*, it is limited to the concerns of culture, ideology, and education; it does not deal with the handling of the economy (or with foreign politics), which was to have been the topic of a different resolution of the same session of the Central Committee of the Chinese Party. Here, too, the overall horizon is the popular desire for economic progress and development. To this end the program of "socialist modernization" has already been inaugurated. And again, for this goal it is "strategically important" to make room for the development of ideology, and especially of ethics: "In building a socialist society . . . the basic task is to help people to become well-educated and self-disciplined socialist citizens with lofty ideals and moral integrity, and to raise the ideological and ethical standards of the whole nation"—all in the interest of "socialist modernization." Where ethical standards are raised, the effect "permeates the whole progress of material advance" and leads to a rise in labor productivity and to new and higher forms of interpersonal relationships that are "characterized by equality, solidarity, friendship, and mutual assistance." Once more, the preponderant question was whether Party members who now exercise power will in fact "whole-heartedly serve the people or behave like bureaucrats and overlords, riding roughshod over the people and abusing power for personal gain." As in Gorbachev's report, this was seen as a question of "renouncing empty talk in favor of practical work." The motivation for such dedicated and unselfish behavior is that the ideal of a Communist society "will always be a source of strength and moral support."

It is clear that the Chinese document, though emphasizing the necessity of the moral progress of people if true socialism and communism are to be attained, does not think in terms of sudden conversion from an unacceptable present practice to better behavior in the future, but rather in terms of development and further perfection. Therefore it emphasizes that "as a higher stage in human moral progress, socialist ethics naturally incorporate all the best elements in the various ethical systems and traditions developed in history," and only "reject all decadent ideology and ethics."

It is in tune with the idea of moral progress and perfection that education should be given the most prominent place among the means to achieve this end. In the early years after the Communist takeover in China, ideological reeducation was a major concern, as is evidenced by *I Was Emperor of China*, written by the last scion of the imperial dynasty. However, "education in ethics" as the road to the attainment and implementation of higher moral standards is the preferred wisdom in the Soviet Union as well as in China. In this respect, Marxism stands in the idealistic tradition of the Enlightenment. The deep anthropological contradiction between *being* and *ought* that Marx had sketched in 1835 was to be overcome by human effort: "If man is to be good, he must be able to be good."

In summary, the original Marxian vision, which is still present in some of the more pragmatic, recent utterances of Marxist officialdom, holds to the need for a moral change in humans. People must move from incumbent egotism to the desired solidarity of socialism, not only in theory and as lip service to the established ideal, but in everyday interpersonal practice. These clearly are pertinent and praiseworthy notions. Because the "hope . . . [in] the living God, who is the Savior of all men" (1 Tim. 4:10) has been ruled out as the motivation of moral change by Marxism, whatever inducement there is must come from earthly agencies. It must necessarily be in the form of a demand made on man by society, either as admonition, command, or legislation. In theological terms, such demands come in the form of the law. Seen in the light of biblical theology, this will continually generate and exacerbate the problem of the transition from theory to practice, because according to the New Testament, the law is unable to produce regeneration and the implementation of its own demands.

The Biblical Response

It has been said that Marxism is a Christian heresy. It has the form of faith, but the content of atheistic humanism. To the extent to which this is true, Marxism will have both strong resemblances to Christian faith and important divergences from it.

Christian theology agrees with Marx's early analysis, that is, his assessment of the fundamental discrepancy in the human between *is* and *ought*. It agrees with his perception of the need for a basic and continuing moral change as well as for constant self-critical awareness. Biblically instructed Christian faith addresses this socially relevant moral task; it is not merely a system of cosmology or a peculiar body of ethnic customs. Indeed, it insists on the centrality of this moral change and does not allow it to disappear periodically in alternating waves of dogmatism and pragmatism.

Jesus, having fed the multitudes, refused to let them consider him only a welcome purveyor of material provisions (John 6:15). Christianity, too, is positively concerned that everyone be provided with the necessities of life. But it also maintains that "man shall not live by bread alone, but by every word that proceeds from the mouth of God" (Matt. 4:4)—a verse sometimes quoted by Marxist leaders, though in its first part only! From the Christian perspective, life is a matter of doing God's will, not of seeking our own welfare. Inbred materialism plays a nasty trick on Marxism at this point, through a half-truth that often poses as the full gospel. Indeed, we need bread, but we cannot settle down when we have it. Material means do not solve moral problems, certainly not when these problems are seen in the dominance of the ego.

Further, Christian faith agrees with Marx in advocating change in individual human life, work, and relationships (i.e., in "local" application). Although Christianity addresses the need for changes in social instructions and legislation, it emphasizes the individual as over against the insistence on changes merely in methods, structures, laws, or personnel, which Marxists so often seem to propagate. Christianity is thoroughly skeptical of lofty global schemes of social salvation, schemes that human beings are notoriously incapable of implementing.

Finally, Christian theology agrees with Marx that such a change in humans must be in the direction of caring for the other person and for humanity. Marx here is quite right in pinpointing the enigma of humanity's moral alienation: the lack of consideration for one's neighbor. There can be no room in Christianity for the cynicism that scoffs at attempts to establish a more just and brotherly society. The moral problems involved in sustaining human life and human association do not go away if they are ignored, but need constant address, in the West no less than in the East. How to engender socially responsible behavior is indeed a problem of immediate relevance in countries whose culture is dominated by the philosophy of the "me generation."

In short, Christian theology supports the concept of concrete conversion. However, biblical faith will also call for a complete conversion in the sense of a turning of the person not merely to his or her neighbor, but also, and primarily, to God. This is fundamental for motivation. Unless God is the goal and guarantor, there is no reason to uphold absolute moral standards. When God is ignored, and change is predicated on human authority alone, moral relativism is inevitable because the power of moral determination is given to individuals or select groups who easily confuse moral standards with their interests. Even in the loftiest of cases, dishonesty for the sake of the cause can become dishonesty for the sake of some personal goal. *And then no redress is possible.* Moral relativism also means the end of moral discourse between all concerned. It cannot be contained, and may finally turn against those who first advocated it with the best of intentions. At this point, Christianity's commitment to justice logically demands absolute moral standards, and these are unthinkable without the authority of God.

The same is true in the field of motivation. The group, the collective, society, and the state are fundamentally insufficient as motivators of unselfishness. The individual will necessarily question the moral demands of others. We are here approaching the problem of whether there can be morality without religion. There seems to be deep wisdom in the so-called motive clause of the Old Testament that endorses ethical demands with divine authority: "You shall not wrong one another, . . . for I am the LORD your God" (Lev. 25:17; cf. Gen. 50:19).

A further problem is how objective moral demands can be subjectivized or internalized. Christian theology has fundamental doubts regarding the ability of education, or the mere presentation of ideas, to produce moral change. Where Marxism pursues this course, it must be seen as still idealistic. Sometimes one gets the impression in socialist countries that the strong forces of nationalism are to be employed as motivators toward the desired moral goal. But that, like the periodic reintroduction of capitalistic principles on the way to socialism, seems to be another attempt to "cross the river on the back of the crocodile"; nationalism certainly does not create the "new man" and the "brotherhood of men," but may indeed easily turn out to be one of the most potent and nasty incarnations of the "old man."

"Administrative measures," or pressuring people into the right kinds of behavior, prove just as futile. The application of force—where, we remember, fundamental moral change is sought—will produce only hypocrisy, unreliability, and widespread window dressing, exactly what was felt to be the problem in the first place. Both education and enforcement are external measures that do not penetrate to the heart and will. It is futile to think that the sinner could accomplish his or her own conversion, or worse, that of others. There will be no reliable conversion to neighbor without a conversion to God. The rediscovery of neighbor without a rediscovery of God is futile; Marxism's atheism plays havoc with its own higher goals.

This is why young Marx, having sketched the problem of man as the only being in creation that does not fulfill its purpose, continued to assert that Christianity is necessary for full moral development. Christianity, above all, addresses the problem of the internalization of the good so that the latter becomes a spontaneous utterance of the believer. Where people encountered Jesus, moral change (as in the story of the tax collector Zacchaeus) came about not by way of demand, but appeared spontaneously, evolving from a necessity of consequence, not of coercion. This is also why Augustine, Bernard, and Calvin refer to the "inner testimony" of the Spirit of God, who authorizes the objective message that is spoken and makes it a person's innermost property. This effects a change in the "heart," that person's center of motivation. This goes beyond moral change as a postulate. It speaks of love as a divine gift, poured out into our hearts (Rom. 5:5). Without it, we will look in vain for moral change that combines self-criticism and an unflinching dedication to the absolute standards of what is right.

The idealism of Marxists is often admirable but their vision and program are fatally flawed by their assessment of egoism and injustice, on the one hand, and forgiveness and change on the other. However sorry the story of Christian faith has sometimes been, it has brought into this world creative men and women of conviction and courage who have profoundly changed the course of life. And it can happen again! For the same God who undergirds life, governs our world, rules the moral order, and directs the course of history is still calling people, in the same way, through the same gospel, into the same resurrection life to serve him and preserve what is good, upright, and honorable in the world. The waves of materialism, practical or theoretical, seem like towering mountains, their power enormous and their appeal irresistible, but always they, too, must crash against the hard realities of life. Men and women were made by God. Despite vaunting idealism on the one side, and gadgets and Porsches on the other, their hearts are always restless until they have found their rest in him.

8

Into the Future

Despite the passage of nineteen hundred years, biblical teaching has not been obliterated. Almost every other event that occurred during that period—every accomplishment, every act of cruelty, every thought or desire—has been forgotten. Time has brought low the mighty, obscured the famous, removed kings and rulers, toppled empires, and transformed civilizations, but it has not effaced the knowledge of Christ nor erased the teaching of his apostles. Neither the gates of hell nor the passage of the years has succeeded in eliminating his church or in wresting from it the biblical teaching on conversion. And that is well for us in the twentieth century, for with all our vaunted progress we still stand in need of the gospel's saving truth as much as any generation ever has.

Yet the church's teaching on conversion has not, as we have seen, been exactly the same in every generation; the characteristics of each age leave their imprint on what the church has taught. When new problems or challenges arise they call forth new answers; they provoke God's people to think afresh about God's truth. At other times, however, the imprint grows out of cultural mindsets that are not commendable, and whose force and direction do change the substance of what is being thought about so that continuity with the past becomes either strained or broken.

Our age is no exception, either in terms of the new challenges or the cultural imprint that colors the understanding of conversion. Two developments seem to have been especially significant. First, this is the age of television. There is probably no clearer illustration of television's influence in the arena of public discourse than what happened to the American presidential debates in 1988. Consider the following comparison. In the mid-nineteenth century, Abraham Lincoln and Stephen Douglas publicly debated one another seven times. The format they followed was short by the standards of their day. Douglas spoke first for an hour. He was rebutted by Lincoln for an hour and a half, and then Douglas concluded with a half-hour rebuttal. By contrast, Governor Dukakis and Vice President Bush debated only twice. In each so-called debate they merely answered reporters' questions. Each answer was limited to two minutes and was followed with a one-minute rebuttal from the opponent. The Lincoln-Douglas debates required what has all but disappeared today: a working attention span, the ability to listen to speeches, to follow coherent argument, to assess ideas; in short, it required of the listeners the ability to think. In the absence of this ability—and it is increasingly absent in the Western nations—Christian faith also is prone to be talked about and to be preached in ways markedly different from those of a century ago. Now the gospel message is often reduced to small pieces and presented in a stream of discontinuous impressions interspersed with comic relief, because the average listener has little patience with material that is not immediately accessible and pleasant to the taste. The trivializing of politics is only a part of the general trivialization of our life and our public discourse; Christianity is not exempt from this scourge. What we now see in the West is a harbinger of things to come in many other parts of the world. Television and modernity are inseparably linked and no country in the Third World can afford to be blasé about the largesse that awaits those who are "modern." Part of that largesse is having a television in the home.

The second major development, which is related to the first, is the growing habit of psychologizing faith. This is a characteristically Western phenomenon, but like television, it seems destined to travel far beyond the Western world. This intrusion of a psychologizing interest shifts the balance from the external to the internal, from what is believed to the act of believing, from what is true to what feels good. It reduces bad natures to bad attitudes and elevates happiness to the place that righteousness once held. This displacement of truth by mood is the exact counterpart to the substitution in television of image for reality. The spinning of fantasies by the one produces a love of fantasies in the other. And that does strange things to the understanding of conversion! The combined effect of these two streams of fantasy often produces, on the one side, a truncated, reduced, and woefully minimal Christian message that appeals to those with a minimal attention span for the realities of life and, on the other, a conversion "event" on the inside of the person. Such an event is thought to be triggered by God, and in it the subjective jigsaw falls into place in a way that produces a sense of peace and fulfillment. It is this fact that has spawned such a widespread interest and confidence in the publicly rendered autobiographies that we call testimonies. In our tired, careworn, and anxious age there seems to be something overwhelmingly compelling about a personal quest for internal peace that ended successfully. How did they do it? What is their secret? Maybe I can find what they have! It is because these questions and desires are not altogether wrong that testimonies have found a happy and unquestioned place in evangelistic practice. Because of the way in which these questions are answered by the format of the testimony and the assumptions that always have to be made when the testimony is rendered, Christian conversion is not always seen in a resoundingly clear and biblical manner. What, then, are the parameters within which this fundamental doctrine should be formulated?

The Gospel Which Is Believed

Christian faith is not primarily about inner contentment, though it may yield that. It is not about happiness, though it may produce that. It is not a shortcut to health or to wealth but to suffering and, in many parts of the world, to serious deprivation. How, then, could we in the West have recast the gospel in terms of contentment and affluence when Jesus said that those who followed him would have to take up, not the pleasurable pursuit of fulfilling themselves, but the cross by which they would be emptied of themselves? It is hard to imagine how the gospel could have been more decisively stood on its head and emptied of its meaning than when it has been misconstrued in these ways.

We need to begin by observing, then, that the gospel is not first and foremost about ourselves. It is not a device for getting what we want or need. It is not a technique for self-improvement or self-accomplishment. It is not a means of tapping our own inner resources. It does not offer itself as a tool for thinking positively about ourselves. It is not about ourselves at all, although we are invited to believe its message.

It is about Christ. It is about the actions of the triune God as he reaches out to sinners who can neither save themselves nor bow before him in submission apart from the working of his grace (Rom. 8:6–8).

So it is when Paul writes to the Ephesians about the gospel. The opening chapter is one long, unbroken sentence in which he draws his readers into a rhapsodic celebration of the actions of the Father, who in his election joined together with his Son those who would later come to him through faith (1:3–6), and of the Son, through whom the Father's plans are known and can be known because of the redemption that is wrought and the forgiveness that the Son achieved (1:7–10), and of the Holy Spirit, who draws Christ's people to him through the gospel and through their belief gives them the assurance of his redemption (1:13–14).

To be sure, all of the elements of this gospel were not apparent every time Paul preached, although when we note how many often were we might have reason to feel chastened. The minimalistic renditions that we often hear today seem as if they come out of a different Bible when compared with what we do know of Paul's practice. Take, for example, his three evangelistic sermons preached in Antioch, Athens, and Lystra (Acts 13:16–41; 17:22–31; 14:15–17). There are no wooden formulae here and that is why on the surface these sermons seem quite different. They are different because the audiences were different. In the first sermon, he was addressing Jews and so began with a review of Jewish history; in the second, at Athens, he was addressing Greeks and so began with the local worship, quoted one of their own poets, and avoided the Jewish history of which they had little knowledge and probably less interest; in the third, in Lystra, which had neither Greek culture nor the Jewish Scriptures, he began with creation, with the experiences of nature and of life with which they were familiar. What is interesting about these sermons, however, is that as different as they are in form, their substance is remarkably similar. They each began with a discussion of history: of the Jews (13:16–23), of the human search for God (17:23–28), and of past religion (14:15–17). In two of the sermons Paul then moved on to show that Jesus is the climax and fulfillment of this history (13:24–25; 17:31); the sermon in Lystra is truncated and was obviously cut short by an agitated crowd. Paul then proclaimed, in the two sermons that are complete, the death and resurrection of Jesus (13:26–29; 17:30–31), forgiveness and justification through him (13:39; 17:31), and God's judgment on those who refuse his Son and his provision (13:40–41; 17:31).

When this common core is pieced together we have in essence Paul's gospel, the gospel he preached in actual evangelistic situations. His starting point was not the need for contentment; he did not restrict gospel meaning to the limited confines of individual need, as consumer theory would surely have demanded. He began with a broad sweep of history, a history that was outside of the sinner. Within these events God has been active, generally so with respect to creation and culture, and particularly so in the life of his people, the Jews. It is objective truth to which Paul points and not subjective need. God was preparing men and women for the coming of his Son and had not been disengaged from life. He acted decisively in the person of the Son, whose coming and death were predicated by the Scriptures, were witnessed to and interpreted by the apostles, but derisively rejected by the Jews who crucified their Messiah. In him, at the cross, God has dealt with sin finally and in a way that no mere human being could do. As God he has taken triumphant action through the Son against all that has marred and broken his world. The work completed, Christ rose from the dead and from him will issue the final judgment to which all will be summoned. What a gospel! And how small, by comparison, is the gospel we often hear today. The contemporary message is circumscribed by inner experience and expects, as a matter of course, that the God of this universe will be pleased, if not privileged, to be able to meet the sinner on his or her own terms! God, it seems, has value to the sinner, is interesting to the sinner, only insofar as he has something to give that the sinner wants—and that is peace and contentment! How strange it is that salvation should even *appear* as the accommodation of God to the sinner when it can be nothing other than the grateful acceptance by the sinner of our great God's kingship and provision of forgiveness.

What plainly is missing is the connection between what we feel internally, the needs that are so intensely present to us, and what Christ has done externally. This connection must be made, for our personal coming to faith is correlative to the work of God in justifying us, ingrafting us into Christ so as to share his death and risen life, adopting us as children and heirs, and sealing us as his own by the gift of the indwelling Holy Spirit. But where this connection is obscured, or where the internal need is allowed to overshadow the external provision, the human side inevitably obscures the divine. Preaching becomes counseling and what is preached is geared not to discovering what God has disclosed but to discovering how we function. When the cross is clearly in view so, too, is the truth that only God can save us; when personal experience is dominant then the truth that only God can save is not. Then the gospel becomes human-centered and in the process the certainty of salvation and the joy of believing evaporate, for neither can be sustained simply on the vagaries of our internal experience. And the majesty, the grace, the breathtaking wonder of what God did in and through his Son is lost. What remains is simply a sinner who was clever enough to get what he or she wanted from God.

The People Who Believe

Technology produces people who make assumptions of omnicompetence, because technology itself is fast becoming omnicompetent. In a technological society it is always assumed that there is an answer to every problem, even if that answer is not immediately apparent. Every problem, it is thought, will one day yield before the combination of technology, sweat, application, and human genius. So it is, perhaps, no surprise that we encounter many people today who also think that the fragmentation of the human spirit is no different and that it, too, will yield before a combination of clever analysis, hard work, and social change.

Our dazzling conquest of the external world, however, does not carry over to a conquest of the internal world. In fact, this is what makes our age so dangerous. Whereas the darker passions and vices of the human spirit once found expression only through bows and arrows, now they can find expression through poison and gas; once warfare was local but now it is often impersonal in its function and whole societies can be smothered, indoctrinated, and controlled. The human spirit may not be more nasty and brutal, but the means for nastiness and brutality have been expanded sometimes beyond our worst nightmares. The omnicompetence that we are close to having in so many areas of our external life should not delude us into thinking that by a process of psychological and spiritual engineering we can also master ourselves. Our great competence in the external world becomes a two-edged sword that can be turned against us as well as used for us.

In evangelical preaching we do not hear the blatant assertion that people can master and save themselves. But in a milder and less obnoxious form the same sort of idea is present in the oft-assumed notion that the sinner has the capacity to trigger the grace of God within himself or herself and so effect conversion. This is one of the extraordinary transformations that has overtaken Christian thinking in the modern period. It was assumed from the time of the Reformation in Europe to the mid-nineteenth century in America that sin had so invaded the personality, had so taken captive heart, mind, and thought, that outside of God's sovereign intervening grace no one would seek God or want him. This is what it means to be under sin. It is what Paul demonstrates is entailed in being sin's captive. It means that "none is righteous, no, not one . . . no one seeks for God . . . no one does good . . . in their paths are ruin and misery . . . there is no fear of God before their eyes" (Rom. 3:10–18). This is what fallen people are like. In an earlier time this understanding was commonly held by all evangelicals, some of whom were Reformed and others of whom were Arminian, but today it is not commonly held. We have lost sight of the biblical understanding of sin and our gospel preaching shows it and is impoverished as a result. We need to recover the full doctrine of sin for ourselves today. We need to turn our backs on the seductions of our omnicompetent culture and affirm with the Bible that men and women in sin are lost and incapable of salvation, incapable of good disposition toward God, his Christ, or his gospel apart from the life-giving work of the Holy Spirit. Self-conversion through one's own initiative, then, like self-justification through one's own works, is an impossibility since fallen human beings are impotent and incompetent in relation to everything that would please

God. Conversion is an act of divine creation in which the agent, as in the natural creation, is and can only be God.

The immediate corollary of this is to see that conversion is a deep and all-encompassing work of God that involves the whole person. Any gospel, by contrast, that pictures God and the sinner being in some kind of cooperative work unitedly bringing about salvation—and much evangelical gospel preaching sounds suspiciously like this despite the ritual deference to the idea of salvation by grace alone—always ends up with a half-baked salvation and a diluted notion of conversion. For the degree to which the sinner contributes anything to his or her salvation except the sin from which he or she needs to be redeemed is the degree to which that work is not divine. And the degree to which it is not divine is the degree to which it is outside God's saving domain. To add human cooperation to the divine work does not produce a richer salvation but a poorer one, not a deeper work but a shallower one. It leaves outside matters that should be brought inside and it presumes to share with God what he has said he will share with no one else, namely, the glory for what he has done.

What happens, then, in a biblical view of conversion is that faith comes to life in the mind as the reality of the truths about Christ, read or heard, begin to take life and to be felt. In some shape or form, these truths center on God's holiness and love, Christ's self-giving for us and in our place, and his triumph over sin, death, and the devil, and our sense of corruption, guilt, misery, and despair. We hear the words of grace. Emotions may well be stirred. Although the perception of spiritual reality is not itself emotional, distress, fear, shame, and joy are at different times often the result. Faith, beginning as knowledge (understanding the truths of Christian faith), blossoms into assent in which the will is now engaged; assent issues in heartfelt trust from whence flows real repentance and the turning from sin to Christ.

This kind of conversion requires a preparation of the heart in the form of a radical humbling for sin. Those who angle the gospel message solely in terms of eliciting a decision will find this notion quite distasteful. They will surely think that this is an unnecessary complication, that it is likely to put off potential converts. They will perhaps note that in the commercial world everything is done to ease a consumer into making the purchase, from the subdued and gentle background music to the way in which the product is packaged to the ease with which credit is extended. Nothing is allowed to stand between a customer and the magical moment when the transaction is made. Why, then, make believing hard when it could be made simple?

The answer, of course, is that we are not choosing between difficulty and simplicity in belief but between genuineness and fraudulence. A genuine belief can be entered into simply but a belief falsely arrived at is not a belief worth having and, without correction, it will not survive the storms of life. In this particular case, we will feel no desire to seek the grace of Christ, the sin-bearer, if we are unaware of the sin that needed to be borne. There is no intrinsic spiritual value in coming to understand our sin; no special merit attaches to this. But its importance lies in the fact that without it we do not know ourselves to be the sinners that we are and hence we will seek to be saved through believing the gospel.

The law was not given to show us that we can live in accord with its requirements; just the reverse! The law lays bare our inner failures, exposes our corrupt motives, reveals in us our persistent drive to replace God and his truth with ourselves and our interests. That is what the law is designed to do. The well-known Californian minister who preached a series of sermons on the Ten Commandments subtitled "How to Feel Good about Yourself" surely missed something quite basic about how the law works and what it does.

To be humbled by the searching truths of the law is not a pleasant experience. It is a necessary one, for it turns us away from our former life of sin and toward Christ. The dismay, emptiness, and revulsion over the past that we feel impels us toward Christ. It prepares us to see him as the only hope of salvation. Christ thus becomes the end of a journey whose passage may be painful but without which the gospel is rendered empty of saving content. This journey must be taken, for in matters of saving faith there are no shortcuts.

How do we know that such a traveler has reached the destination, that the law has done its work and brought the sinner to Christ? The answer is twofold. First, it comes through the assurance wrought by the Holy Spirit. Whether this assurance is a part of faith or a consequence of faith is a minor consideration; what is important is that it be affirmed, against traditional Roman Catholicism, that assurance is the birthright of the child of God. God wants us to have the certain consciousness of our faith. He wants us to know that despite all of the experiences in life that call into question his existence, his love and good will, his holiness, he is in fact unchanged and eternally bound in love to all who are his in Christ.

Second, the test of conversion is a life of convertedness. The parable of the soil warns us that enthusiasm for things Christian is not necessarily evidence of spiritual rebirth. Decisions can be predicted on faulty information or incomplete knowledge. Or these may be decisions whose action is devoid of that heartfelt trust in Christ without which salvation cannot take place, that by ourselves they offer no evidence of conversion. The only way faith is evidenced is in the presence of works.

The test of conversion, then, is whether a sinner continues to see sin as displeasing to God and continues to turn from it, continues to seek Christ and trust him for life, forgiveness, grace, and guidance. It is whether believing in Christ leads to following him by denying ourselves and daily taking up our cross and following him, seeking his kingdom above our interests, loving and serving his people because of his love for us. It is whether the graces of Christian character begin to appear. It is whether we begin to learn how to live in God's world on his terms, recognizing him as the sovereign creator and sustainer of all, thankfully accepting from him the good gifts and experiences he gives us and accepting the disappointments with the kind of submission that can come only from a deep sense of his abiding goodness. When conversion leads to a love of God and his glory and a commitment to serve and honor him in all that we do, then the conversion is genuine. It is in these ways, the ways of the life of faith, that we are given the only evidence of the reality of a person's profession of faith.

Christian faith is never more than one generation from extinction, humanly speaking, and so each generation has to take care to ensure that the faith is preserved in its full integrity. This is no easy task, for as much as we long for hiding places, safe havens where we are neither pressured by life's pains and perplexities nor exposed to evil and error, we find none, except in him who loved us and gave himself for us, the righteous for the unrighteous, that we might know God who abides forever. And our painful limitations and vulnerabilities only cause us with greater determination to find in God our strength and hope. When we struggle to learn, preserve, and live Christian faith, we will no longer be doing so merely humanly.

Bibliography

Alexander, Archibald. *Thoughts on Religious Experience.* Edinburgh: Banner of Truth, 1967.

Alfoldi, Andras. *The Conversion of Constantine and Pagan Rome.* Translated by Harold Mattingly. Oxford: Clarendon, 1948.

Ali, Abdullah Yusuf. *The Meaning of the Glorious Qur'an.* Cairo: Dar al-Kitab al-Masri, 1938.

Baillie, John. *Baptism and Conversion.* New York: Scribner, 1963.

Barclay, William. *Turning to God: A Study of Conversion in the Book of Acts.* Philadelphia: Westminster, 1964.

Barnhart, Joe E. *The New Birth: A Naturalistic View of Religious Conversion.* Macon, GA: Mercer University Press, 1981.

Barrett, David. *Schism and Renewal in Africa: An Analysis of Six Thousand Contemporary Religious Movements.* Nairobi: Oxford University Press, 1968.

Baxter, Richard. *A Call to the Unconverted.* Princeton: Princeton University Press, 1827.

———. *A Treatise on Conversion.* New York: American Tract Society, n.d.

Bella, Robert, and Philip E. Hammond. *Varieties of Civil Religion.* New York: Harper and Row, 1981.

Berger, Peter L. *A Rumor of Angels.* Garden City, NY: Harper and Row, 1970.

Best, W. E. *Regeneration and Conversion.* Grand Rapids: Baker, 1975.

Bockmuehl, Klaus. *The Challenge of Marxism.* Leicester: Inter-Varsity, 1980.

Brandon, Owen. *The Battle for the Soul: Aspects of Religious Conversion.* Philadelphia: Westminster, 1959.

Buckland, R. *Children and God.* London: Scripture Union, 1988.

Caldwell, Patricia. *The Puritan Conversion Narrative: The Beginnings of American Expression.* Cambridge: Cambridge University Press, 1983.

Chesterton, G. K. *The Catholic Church and Conversion.* New York: Macmillan, 1961.

Citron, Bernhard. *New Birth: A Study of the Evangelical Doctrine of Conversion in the Protestant Fathers.* Edinburgh: University Press, 1951.

Colson, Charles W. *Born Again.* Tappan, NJ: Chosen, 1976.

Conn, Walter E., ed. *Conversion: Perspectives on Personal and Social Transformation.* New York: Alba House, 1978.

Costas, Orlando. *The Church and Its Mission: A Shattering Critique from the Third World.* Wheaton: Tyndale House, 1974.

Dumoulin, H. *Zen Enlightenment: Origins and Meaning.* Translated by J. C. Mavaldo. New York: Weatherhill, 1979.

Dunn, J. D. G. *Baptism in the Holy Spirit.* London: SCM, 1970.

Eadie, John W. *The Conversion of Constantine.* New York: Holt, Rinehart, and Winston, 1971.

Edwards, Jonathan. *The Treatise on Religious Affections.* New York: Yale University Press, 1959.

Elwood, D. *Church and Sects in the Philippines.* Dumaguette, Philippines: Silliman University Press, 1968.

Engel, James F., and H. W. Norton. *What's Gone Wrong with the Harvest.* Grand Rapids: Zondervan, 1975.

Erickson, E. *Identity, Youth and Crisis.* New York: Naten, 1968.

Eusden, John Dykstra. *Zen and Christian: The Journey Between.* New York: Crossroad, 1981.

Ferm, Robert O. *The Psychology of Christian Conversion*. Westwood, NJ: Revell, 1959.

Gaventa, B. R. *From Darkness to Light: Aspects of Conversion in the New Testament*. Philadelphia: Fortress, 1986.

Gillespie, Virgil B. *Religious Conversion and Personal Identity: How and Why People Change*. Birmingham, AL: Religious Education Press, 1979.

Grayzel, Solomon. *A History of the Jews*. Philadelphia: Jewish Publication Society of America, 1968.

Green, E. M. B. *Evangelism in the Early Church*. London: Hodder and Stoughton, 1970.

Green, Richard. *The Conversion of John Wesley*. London: Epworth, 1937.

Gritsch, Eric W. *Born-Againism: Perspectives on a Movement*. Philadelphia: Fortress, 1982.

Guardini, Romano. *The Conversion of Augustine*. Translated by Elinor Brieks. Westminster, MD: Newman Press, 1960.

Harran, Marilyn J. *Luther on Conversion: The Early Years*. Ithaca, NY: Cornell University Press, 1983.

Hick, John. *God and the Universe of Faiths*. New York: St. Martin, 1974.

Holladay, William C. *The Root Subh in the Old Testament*. Leiden: E. J. Brill, 1958.

James, William. *The Varieties of Religious Experience*. New York: Modern Library, 1936.

Johnson, Cedric B. *Christian Conversion: Biblical and Psychological Perspectives*. Grand Rapids: Zondervan, 1982.

Jones, E. Stanley. *Conversion*. New York: Abingdon, 1959.

Kasdorff, Hans. *Christian Conversion in Context*. Scottdale, PA: Herald, 1980.

Kearney, Michael. *World View*. Novato, CA: Chandler and Sharp, 1984.

Kerr, Hugh T., and John M. Mulder. *Conversions: The Christian Experience*. Grand Rapids: Eerdmans, 1983.

Kim, Seyoon. *The Origin of Paul's Gospel*. Grand Rapids: Eerdmans, 1982.

King, John O. *The Iron of Melancholy: Structures of Spiritual Conversion.* Middletown, CT: Wesleyan University Press, 1983.

Krailsheimer, A. J. *Conversion.* London: SCM, 1980.

Linder, Robert, and Richard Pierard. *Twilight of the Saints: Biblical Christianity and Civil Religion in America.* Downers Grove: InterVarsity, 1978.

Lohfink, Gerhard. *The Conversion of St. Paul: Narrative and History in Acts.* Chicago: Franciscan Herald Press, 1976.

Machen, J. Gresham. *The Origin of Paul's Religion.* Grand Rapids: Eerdmans, 1965.

McFarland, H. M. *The Rush Hour of the Gods.* New York: Macmillan, 1967.

McLellan, D. *Karl Marx: His Life and Thought.* New York: Harper, 1977.

Miller, Glenn T. *The Rise of Evangelical Calvinism: A Study in Jonathan Edwards and the Puritan Tradition.* New York: Miller, 1971.

Newbigin, Lesslie. *The Finality of Christ.* Richmond: John Knox, 1969.

Nock, Arthur D. *Conversion: The Old and New in Religion from Alexander the Great to Augustine of Hippo.* Oxford: Clarendon, 1933.

Peachey, E. T. *A History of Zen Buddhism.* London: Faber and Faber, 1963.

Pettit, Norman. *The Heart Prepared: Grace and Conversion in Puritan Spiritual Life.* New Haven: Yale University Press, 1966.

Richardson, Herbert, ed. *New Religions and Mental Health: Understanding the Issues.* New York: Edwin Mellen Press, 1980.

Richey, Russell, and Donald Jones, eds. *American Civil Religion.* New York: Harper and Row, 1974.

Routley, Erik. *Conversion.* Philadelphia: Fortress, 1977.

Suzuki, D. T. *An Introduction to Zen Buddhism.* New York: Philosophical Library, 1949.

———. *Zen and Japanese Buddhism.* Tokyo: Japan Travel Bureau, 1958.

The Willowbank Report: Gospel and Culture. Lausanne Occasional Papers, No. 2. Wheaton: Lausanne Committee for World Evangelization, 1978.

Tillich, Paul. *Christianity and the Encounter of the World Religion.* New York: Columbia University Press, 1963.

Wells, David F. *God the Evangelist: How the Holy Spirit Works to Bring Men and Women to Faith.* Grand Rapids: Eerdmans, 1987.

Index

David F. Wells is the Distinguished Research Professor at Gordon-Conwell Theological Seminary. He has eighteen books to his credit, including *God the Evangelist: How the Holy Spirit Works to Bring Men and Women to Faith*.

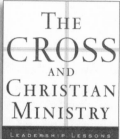

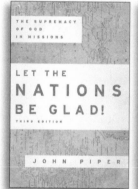
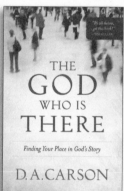
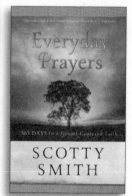